Reinforcement Learning

With Open AI, TensorFlow and Keras Using Python

■■■

Abhishek Nandy

Manisha Biswas

Apress®

Reinforcement Learning

Abhishek Nandy
Kolkata, West Bengal, India

Manisha Biswas
North 24 Parganas, West Bengal, India

ISBN-13 (pbk): 978-1-4842-3284-2
https://doi.org/10.1007/978-1-4842-3285-9

ISBN-13 (electronic): 978-1-4842-3285-9

Library of Congress Control Number: 2017962867

Cover image by Freepik (`www.freepik.com`)

Managing Director: Welmoed Spahr
Editorial Director: Todd Green
Acquisitions Editor: Celestin Suresh John
Development Editor: Matthew Moodie
Technical Reviewer: Avirup Basu
Coordinating Editor: Sanchita Mandal
Copy Editor: Kezia Endsley
Compositor: SPi Global
Indexer: SPi Global
Artist: SPi Global

Distributed to the book trade worldwide by Springer Science+Business Media New York, 233 Spring Street, 6th Floor, New York, NY 10013. Phone 1-800-SPRINGER, fax (201) 348-4505, e-mail `orders-ny@springer-sbm.com`, or visit `www.springeronline.com`. Apress Media, LLC is a California LLC and the sole member (owner) is Springer Science + Business Media Finance Inc (SSBM Finance Inc). SSBM Finance Inc is a **Delaware** corporation.

For information on translations, please e-mail `rights@apress.com`, or visit `http://www.apress.com/rights-permissions`.

Apress titles may be purchased in bulk for academic, corporate, or promotional use. eBook versions and licenses are also available for most titles. For more information, reference our Print and eBook Bulk Sales web page at `http://www.apress.com/bulk-sales`.

Any source code or other supplementary material referenced by the author in this book is available to readers on GitHub via the book's product page, located at `www.apress.com/978-1-4842-3284-2`. For more detailed information, please visit `http://www.apress.com/source-code`.

Printed on acid-free paper

Contents

About the Authors

Abhishek Nandy has a B.Tech. in information technology and considers himself a constant learner. He is a Microsoft MVP in the Windows platform, an Intel Black Belt Developer, as well as an Intel software innovator. Abhishek has a keen interest in artificial intelligence, IoT, and game development. He is currently serving as an application architect at an IT firm and consults in AI and IoT, as well does projects in AI, Machine Learning, and deep learning. He is also an AI trainer and drives the technical part of Intel AI student developer program. He was involved in the first Make in India initiative, where he was among the top 50 innovators and was trained in IIMA.

Manisha Biswas has a B.Tech. in information technology and currently works as a software developer at InSync Tech-Fin Solutions Ltd in Kolkata, India. She is involved in several areas of technology, including web development, IoT, soft computing, and artificial intelligence. She is an Intel Software innovator and was awarded the Shri Dewang Mehta IT Awards 2016 by NASSCOM, a certificate of excellence for top academic scores. She very recently formed a "Women in Technology" community in Kolkata, India to empower women to learn and explore new technologies. She likes to invent things, create something new, and invent a new look for the old things. When not in front of her terminal, she is an explorer, a foodie, a doodler, and a dreamer. She is always very passionate to share her knowledge and ideas with others. She is following her passion currently by sharing her experiences with the community so that others can learn, which lead her to become Google Women Techmakers, Kolkata Chapter Lead.

About the Technical Reviewer

Avirup Basu is an IoT application developer at Prescriber360 Solutions. He is a researcher in robotics and has published papers through the IEEE.

Acknowledgments

I want to dedicate this book to my parents.

—Abhishek Nandy

I want to dedicate this book to my mom and dad. Thank you to my teachers and my co-author, Abhishek Nandy. Thanks also to Abhishek Sur, who mentors me at work and helps me adapt to new technologies. I would also like to dedicate this book to my company, InSync Tech-Fin Solutions Ltd., where I started my career and have grown professionally.

—Manisha Biswas

Introduction

This book is primarily based on a Machine Learning subset known as *Reinforcement Learning*. We cover the basics of Reinforcement Learning with the help of the Python programming language and touch on several aspects, such as Q learning, MDP, RL with Keras, and OpenAI Gym and OpenAI Environment, and also cover algorithms related to RL.

Users need a basic understanding of programming in Python to benefit from this book.

The book is meant for people who want to get into Machine Learning and learn more about Reinforcement Learning.

CHAPTER 1

■ ■ ■

Reinforcement Learning Basics

This chapter is a brief introduction to Reinforcement Learning (RL) and includes some key concepts associated with it.

In this chapter, we talk about Reinforcement Learning as a core concept and then define it further. We show a complete flow of how Reinforcement Learning works. We discuss exactly where Reinforcement Learning fits into artificial intelligence (AI). After that we define key terms related to Reinforcement Learning. We start with agents and then touch on environments and then finally talk about the connection between agents and environments.

What Is Reinforcement Learning?

We use Machine Learning to constantly improve the performance of machines or programs over time. The simplified way of implementing a process that improves machine performance with time is using Reinforcement Learning (RL). Reinforcement Learning is an approach through which intelligent programs, known as *agents*, work in a known or unknown environment to constantly adapt and learn based on giving points. The feedback might be positive, also known as *rewards*, or negative, also called *punishments*. Considering the agents and the environment interaction, we then determine which action to take.

In a nutshell, Reinforcement Learning is based on rewards and punishments. Some important points about Reinforcement Learning:

- It differs from normal Machine Learning, as we do not look at training datasets.

- Interaction happens not with data but with environments, through which we depict real-world scenarios.

© Abhishek Nandy and Manisha Biswas 2018
A. Nandy and M. Biswas, *Reinforcement Learning*,
https://doi.org/10.1007/978-1-4842-3285-9_1

- As Reinforcement Learning is based on environments, many parameters come in to play. It takes lots of information to learn and act accordingly.

- Environments in Reinforcement Learning are real-world scenarios that might be 2D or 3D simulated worlds or game-based scenarios.

- Reinforcement Learning is broader in a sense because the environments can be large in scale and there might be a lot of factors associated with them.

- The objective of Reinforcement Learning is to reach a goal.

- Rewards in Reinforcement Learning are obtained from the environment.

The Reinforcement Learning cycle is depicted in Figure 1-1 with the help of a robot.

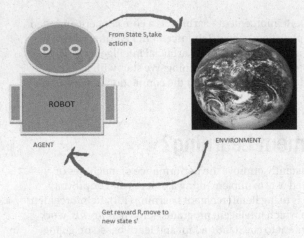

Figure 1-1. *Reinforcement Learning cycle*

A maze is a good example that can be studied using Reinforcement Learning, in order to determine the exact right moves to complete the maze (see Figure 1-2).

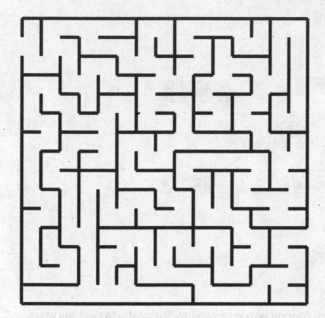

Figure 1-2. *Reinforcement Learning can be applied to mazes*

In Figure 1-3, we are applying Reinforcement Learning and we call it the Reinforcement Learning box because within its vicinity the process of RL works. RL starts with an intelligent program, known as agents, and when they interact with environments, there are rewards and punishments associated. An environment can be either known or unknown to the agents. The agents take actions to move to the next state in order to maximize rewards.

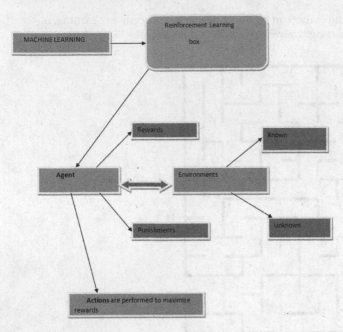

Figure 1-3. *Reinforcement Learning flow*

In the maze, the centralized concept is to keep moving. The goal is to clear the maze and reach the end as quickly as possible.

The following concepts of Reinforcement Learning and the working scenario are discussed later this chapter.

- The agent is the intelligent program

- The environment is the maze

- The state is the place in the maze where the agent is

- The action is the move we take to move to the next state

- The reward is the points associated with reaching a particular state. It can be positive, negative, or zero

We use the maze example to apply concepts of Reinforcement Learning. We will be describing the following steps:

1. The concept of the maze is given to the agent.

2. There is a task associated with the agent and Reinforcement Learning is applied to it.

3. The agent receives (a-1) reinforcement for every move it makes from one state to other.

4. There is a reward system in place for the agent when it moves from one state to another.

The rewards predictions are made iteratively, where we update the value of each state in a maze based on the value of the best subsequent state and the immediate reward obtained. This is called the *update rule*.

The constant movement of the Reinforcement Learning process is based on decision-making.

Reinforcement Learning works on a trial-and-error basis because it is very difficult to predict which action to take when it is in one state. From the maze problem itself, you can see that in order get the optimal path for the next move, you have to weigh a lot of factors. It is always on the basis of state action and rewards. For the maze, we have to compute and account for probability to take the step.

The maze also does not consider the reward of the previous step; it is specifically considering the move to the next state. The concept is the same for all Reinforcement Learning processes.

Here are the steps of this process:

1. We have a problem.

2. We have to apply Reinforcement Learning.

3. We consider applying Reinforcement Learning as a Reinforcement Learning box.

4. The Reinforcement Learning box contains all essential components needed for applying the Reinforcement Learning process.

5. The Reinforcement Learning box contains agents, environments, rewards, punishments, and actions.

Reinforcement Learning works well with intelligent program agents that give rewards and punishments when interacting with an environment.

The interaction happens between the agents and the environments, as shown in Figure 1-4.

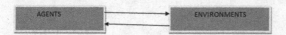

Figure 1-4. *Interaction between agents and environments*

From Figure 1-4, you can see that there is a direct interaction between the agents and its environments. This interaction is very important because through these exchanges, the agent adapts to the environments. When a Machine Learning program, robot, or Reinforcement Learning program starts working, the agents are exposed to known or unknown environments and the Reinforcement Learning technique allows the agents to interact and adapt according to the environment's features.

Accordingly, the agents work and the Reinforcement Learning robot learns. In order to get to a desired position, we assign rewards and punishments.

Now, the program has to work around the optimal path to get maximum rewards if it fails (that is, it takes punishments or receives negative points). In order to reach a new position, which also is known as a *state*, it must perform what we call an *action*.

To perform an action, we implement a function, also known as a *policy*. A policy is therefore a function that does some work.

Faces of Reinforcement Learning

As you see from the Venn diagram in Figure 1-5, Reinforcement Learning sits at the intersection of many different fields of science.

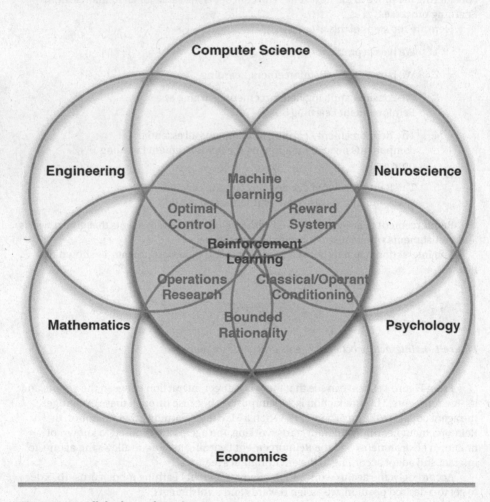

Figure 1-5. *All the faces of Reinforcement Learning*

The intersection points reveal a very strong feature of Reinforcement Learning—it shows the science of decision-making. If we have two paths and have to decide which path to take so that some point is met, a scientific decision-making process can be designed.

Reinforcement Learning is the fundamental science of optimal decision-making.

If we focus on the computer science part of the Venn diagram in Figure 1-5, we see that if we want to learn, it falls under the category of Machine Learning, which is specifically mapped to Reinforcement Learning.

Reinforcement Learning can be applied to many different fields of science. In engineering, we have devices that focus mostly on optimal control. In neuroscience, we are concerned with how the brain works as a stimulant for making decisions and study the reward system that works on the brain (the dopamine system).

Psychologists can apply Reinforcement Learning to determine how animals make decisions. In mathematics, we have a lot of data applying Reinforcement Learning in operations research.

The Flow of Reinforcement Learning

Figure 1-6 connects agents and environments.

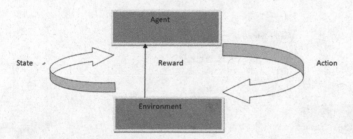

Figure 1-6. RL structure

The interaction happens from one state to another. The exact connection starts between an agent and the environment. Rewards are happening on a regular basis.

We take appropriate actions to move from one state to another.

The key points of consideration after going through the details are the following:

- The Reinforcement Learning cycle works in an interconnected manner.

- There is distinct communication between the agent and the environment.

- The distinct communication happens with rewards in mind.

- The object or robot moves from one state to another.

- An action is taken to move from one state to another

Figure 1-7 simplifies the interaction process.

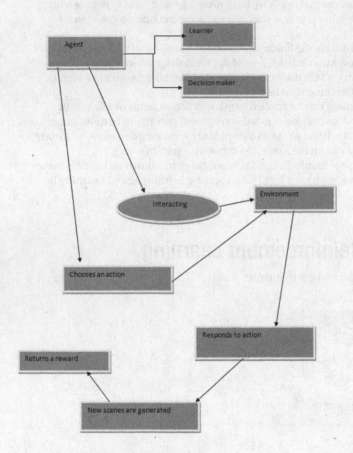

Figure 1-7. *The entire interaction process*

An agent is always learning and finally makes a decision. An agent is a learner, which means there might be different paths. When the agent starts training, it starts to adapt and intelligently learns from its surroundings.

The agent is also a decision maker because it tries to take an action that will get it the maximum reward.

When the agent starts interacting with the environment, it can choose an action and respond accordingly.

From then on, new scenes are created. When the agent changes from one place to another in an environment, every change results in some kind of modification. These changes are depicted as *scenes*. The transition that happens in each step helps the agent solve the Reinforcement Learning problem more effectively.

Let's look at another scenario of state transitioning, as shown in Figures 1-8 and 1-9.

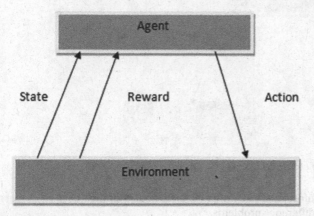

Figure 1-8. *Scenario of state changes*

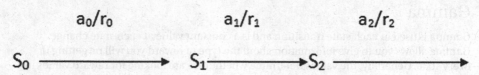

Figure 1-9. *The state transition process*

Learn to choose actions that maximize the following:

$$r0 + \gamma r1 + \gamma 2r2 + \ldots\ldots\ldots\ldots\ldots \text{ where } 0 < \gamma < 1$$

At each state transition, the reward is a different value, hence we describe reward with varying values in each step, such as r0, r1, r2, etc. Gamma (γ) is called a *discount factor* and it determines what future reward types we get:

- A gamma value of 0 means the reward is associated with the current state only

- A gamma value of 1 means that the reward is long-term

Different Terms in Reinforcement Learning

Now we cover some common terms associated with Reinforcement Learning.

There are two constants that are important in this case—gamma (γ) and lambda (λ), as shown in Figure 1-10.

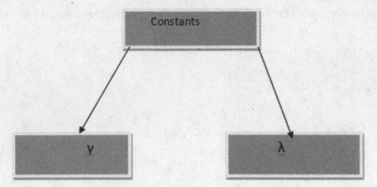

Figure 1-10. *Showing values of constants*

Gamma is common in Reinforcement Learning problems but lambda is used generally in terms of temporal difference problems.

Gamma

Gamma is used in each state transition and is a constant value at each state change. Gamma allows you to give information about the type of reward you will be getting in every state. Generally, the values determine whether we are looking for reward values in each state only (in which case, it's 0) or if we are looking for long-term reward values (in which case it's 1).

Lambda

Lambda is generally used when we are dealing with temporal difference problems. It is more involved with predictions in successive states.

Increasing values of lambda in each state shows that our algorithm is learning fast. The faster algorithm yields better results when using Reinforcement Learning techniques.

As you'll learn later, temporal differences can be generalized to what we call TD(Lambda). We discuss it in greater depth later.

Interactions with Reinforcement Learning

Let's now talk about Reinforcement Learning and its interactions. As shown in Figure 1-11, the interactions between the agent and the environment occur with a reward. We need to take an action to move from one state to another.

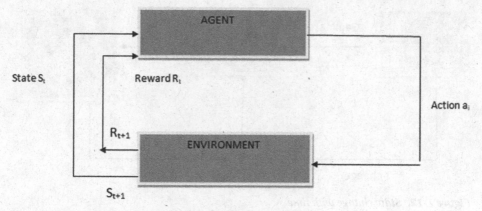

Figure 1-11. *Reinforcement Learning interactions*

Reinforcement Learning is a way of implementing how to map situations to actions so as to maximize and find a way to get the highest rewards.

The machine or robot is not told which actions to take, as with other forms of Machine Learning, but instead the machine must discover which actions yield the maximum reward by trying them.

In the most interesting and challenging cases, actions affect not only the immediate reward but also the next situation and all subsequent rewards.

RL Characteristics

We talk about characteristics next. The characteristics are generally what the agent does to move to the next state. The agent considers which approach works best to make the next move.

The two characteristics are

- Trial and error search.

- Delayed reward.

As you probably have gathered, Reinforcement Learning works on three things combined:

(S,A,R)

Where *S* represents state, *A* represents action, and *R* represents reward.

If you are in a state *S*, you perform an action *A* so that you get a reward *R* at time frame *t+1*. Now, the most important part is when you move to the next state. In this case, we do not use the reward we just earned to decide where to move next. Each transition has a unique reward and no reward from any previous state is used to determine the next move. See Figure 1-12.

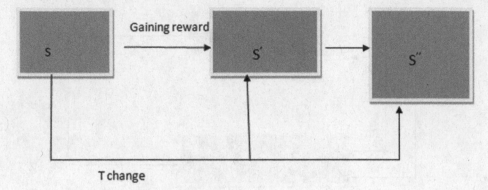

Figure 1-12. State change with time

The T change (the time frame) is important in terms of Reinforcement Learning. Every occurrence of what we do is always a combination of what we perform in terms of states, actions, and rewards. See Figure 1-13.

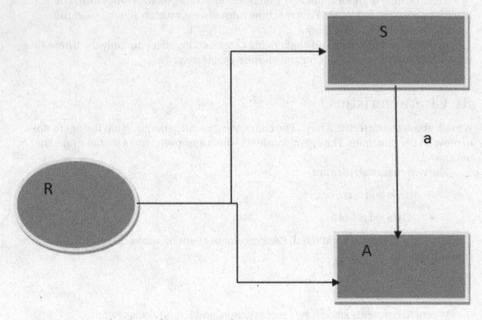

Figure 1-13. Another way of representing the state transition

How Reward Works

A *reward* is some motivator we receive when we transition from one state to another. It can be points, as in a video game. The more we train, the more accurate we become, and the greater our reward.

Agents

In terms of Reinforcement Learning, agents are the software programs that make intelligent decisions. Agents should be able to perceive what is happening in the environment. Here are the basic steps of the agents:

1. When the agent can perceive the environment, it can make better decisions.

2. The decision the agents take results in an action.

3. The action that the agents perform must be the best, the optimal, one.

Software agents might be autonomous or they might work together with other agents or with people. Figure 1-14 shows how the agent works.

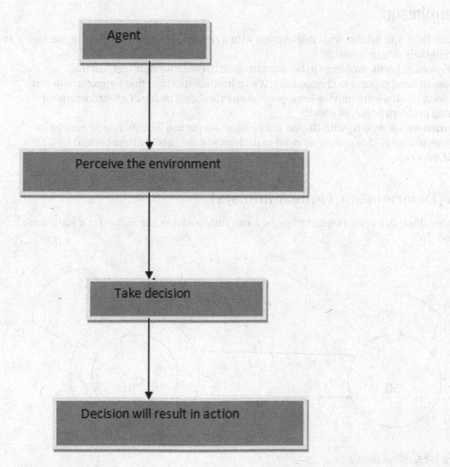

Figure 1-14. The flow of the environment

RL Environments

The environments in the Reinforcement Learning space are comprised of certain factors that determine the impact on the Reinforcement Learning agent. The agent must adapt accordingly to the environment. These environments can be 2D worlds or grids or even a 3D world.

Here are some important features of environments:

- Deterministic
- Observable
- Discrete or continuous
- Single or multiagent.

Deterministic

If we can infer and predict what will happen with a certain scenario in the future, we say the scenario is deterministic.

It is easier for RL problems to be deterministic because we don't rely on the decision-making process to change state. It's an immediate effect that happens with state transitions when we are moving from one state to another. The life of a Reinforcement Learning problem becomes easier.

When we are dealing with RL, the state model we get will be either deterministic or non-deterministic. That means we need to understand the mechanisms behind how DFA and NDFA work.

DFA (Deterministic Finite Automata)

DFA goes through a finite number of steps. It can only perform one action for a state. See Figure 1-15.

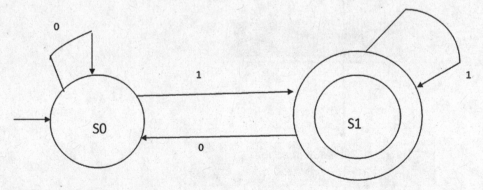

Figure 1-15. *Showing DFA*

We are showing a state transition from a start state to a final state with the help of a diagram. It is a simple depiction where we can say that, with some input value that is assumed as 1 and 0, the state transition occurs. The self-loop is created when it gets a value and stays in the same state.

NDFA (Nondeterministic Finite Automaton)

If we are working in a scenario where we don't know exactly which state a machine will move into, this is a case of NDFA. See Figure 1-16.

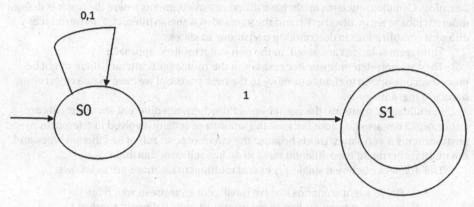

Figure 1-16. *NDFA*

The working principle of the state diagram in Figure 1-16 can be explained as follows. In NDFA the issue is when we are transitioning from one state to another, there is more than one option available, as we can see in Figure 1-16. From State S0 after getting an input such as 0, it can stay in state S0 or move to state S1. There is decision-making involved here, so it becomes difficult to know which action to take.

Observable

If we can say that the environment around us is fully observable, we have a perfect scenario for implementing Reinforcement Learning.

An example of perfect observability is a chess game. An example of partial observability is a poker game, where some of the cards are unknown to any one player.

Discrete or Continuous

If there is more than one choice for transitioning to the next state, that is a continuous scenario. When there are a limited number of choices, that's called a discrete scenario.

Single Agent and Multiagent Environments

Solutions in Reinforcement Learning can be of single agent types or multiagent types.

Let's take a look at multiagent Reinforcement Learning first.

When we are dealing with complex problems, we use multiagent Reinforcement Learning. Complex problems might have different environments where the agent is doing different jobs to get involved in RL and the agent also wants to interact. This introduces different complications in determining transitions in states.

Multiagent solutions are based on the non-deterministic approach.

They are non-deterministic because when the multiagents interact, there might be more than one option to change or move to the next state and we have to make decisions based on that ambiguity.

In multiagent solutions, the agent interactions between different environments are enormous. They are enormous because the amount of activity involved in references to environments is very large. This is because the environments might be different types and the multiagents might have different tasks to do in each state transition.

The difference between single-agent and multiagent solutions are as follows:

- Single-agent scenarios involve intelligent software in which the interaction happens in one environment only. If there is another environment simultaneously, it cannot interact with the first environment.

- When there is little bit of convergence in Reinforcement Learning. Convergence is when the agent needs to interact far more often in different environments to make a decision. This scenario is tackled by multiagents, as single agents cannot tackle convergence. Single agents cannot tackle convergence because it connects to other environments when there might be different scenarios involving simultaneous decision-making.

- Multiagents have dynamic environments compared to single agents. Dynamic environments can involve changing environments in the places to interact with.

Figure 1-17 shows the single-agent scenario.

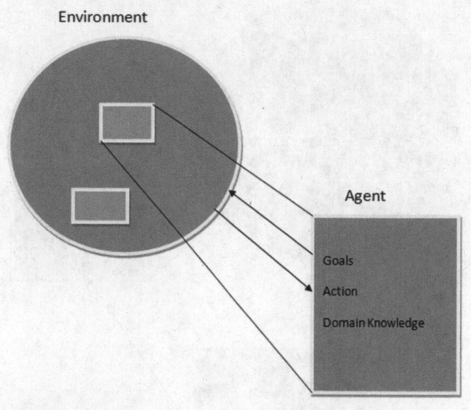

Figure 1-17. *Single agent*

Figure 1-18 shows how multiagents work. There is an interaction between two agents in order to make the decision.

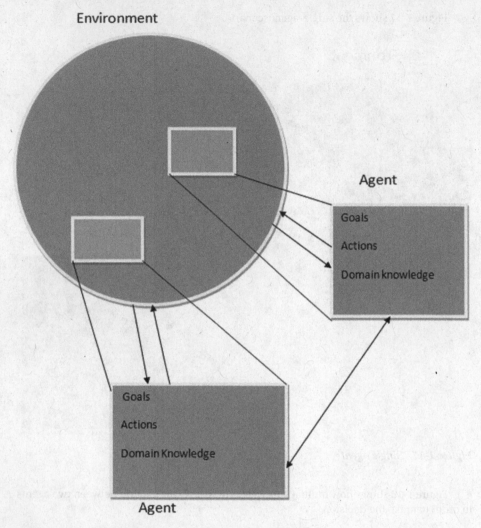

Figure 1-18. *Multiagent scenario*

Conclusion

This chapter touched on the basics of Reinforcement Learning and covered some key concepts. We covered states and environments and how the structure of Reinforcement Learning looks.

We also touched on the different kinds of interactions and learned about single-agent and multiagent solutions.

The next chapter covers algorithms and discusses the building blocks of Reinforcement Learning.

CHAPTER 2

■ ■ ■

RL Theory and Algorithms

This chapter covers how Reinforcement Learning works and explains the concepts behind it, including the different algorithms that form the basis of Reinforcement Learning.

The chapter explains these algorithms, but to start with, you will learn why Reinforcement Learning can be hard and see some different scenarios. The chapter also covers different ways that Reinforcement Learning can be implemented.

Along the way, the chapter formulates the Markov Decision Process (MDP) and describes it. The chapter also covers SARSA and touches on temporal differences. Then, the chapter touches on Q Learning and dynamic programming.

Theoretical Basis of Reinforcement Learning

This section touches on the theoretical basis of Reinforcement Learning. Figure 2-1 shows how you are going to implement MDP, which is described later.

© Abhishek Nandy and Manisha Biswas 2018
A. Nandy and M. Biswas, *Reinforcement Learning*,
https://doi.org/10.1007/978-1-4842-3285-9_2

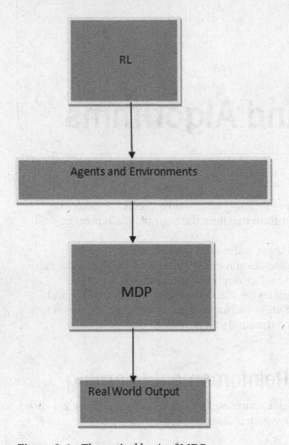

Figure 2-1. *Theoretical basis of MDP*

Environments in Reinforcement Learning are represented by the Markov Decision Process (discussed later in this chapter).

- SS is a finite set of states. AA is a finite set of actions.

- T:S×A×S→[0,1]T:S×A×S→[0,1] is a transition model that maps (state, action, state) triples to probabilities.

- T(s,a,s′)T(s,a,s′) is the probability that you'll land in state s′s′ if you were in state ss and took action aa.

In terms of conditional probabilities, the following is true:

$$T(s,a,s')=P(s'|s,a)T(s,a,s')=P(s'|s,a)$$

$R:S{\times}S{\rightarrow}RR:S{\times}S{\rightarrow}R$ is a reward function that gives a real number that represents the amount of reward (or punishment) the environment will grant for a state transition. $R(s,s')R(s,s')$ is the reward received after transitioning to state $s's'$ from state ss.

If the transition model is known to the agent, i.e., the agent knows where it would probably go from where it stands, it's fairly easy for the agent to know how to act in a way that maximizes its expected utility from its experience with the environment.

We can define the expected utility for the agent to be the accumulated rewards it gets throughout its experience with the environment. If the agent goes through the states $s0,s1,\ldots,sn-1,sns0,s1,\ldots,sn-1,sn$, you could formally define its expected utility as follows:

$$\Sigma nt=1{\gamma}tE[R(st-1,st)]\Sigma t=1n{\gamma}tE[R(st-1,st)]$$

where $\gamma\gamma$ is a discount factor used to decrease the values (and hence the importance) of past rewards, and EE is the expected value.

The problem arises when the agents have no clue about the probabilistic model behind the transitions, and this where RL comes in. The RL problem can formally be defined now as the problem of learning a set of parameters in order to maximize the expected utility.

RL comes in two flavors:

- *Model-based:* The agent attempts to sample and learn the probabilistic model and use it to determine the best actions it can take. In this flavor, the set of parameters that was vaguely referred to is the MDP model.

- *Model-free:* The agent doesn't bother with the MDP model and instead attempts to develop a control function that looks at the state and decides the best action to take. In that case, the parameters to be learned are the ones that define the control function.

Where Reinforcement Learning Is Used

This section discusses the different fields of Reinforcement Learning, as shown in Figure 2-2.

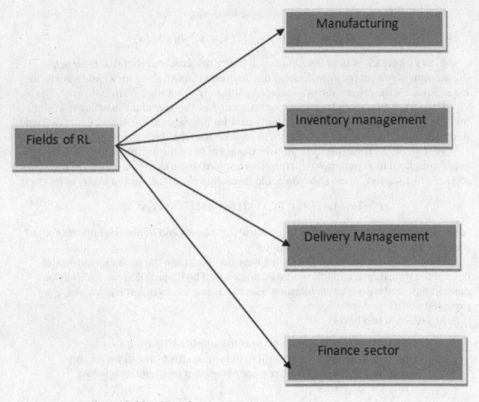

Figure 2-2. *Different fields of Reinforcement Learning*

Manufacturing

In manufacturing, factory robots use Reinforcement Learning to move an object from one box and then keep it in another container.

If it fails or finds success upon delivering, the robot remembers the object and learns again, with the end result to get the best results with the greatest accuracy.

Inventory Management

In terms of inventory management, Reinforcement Learning can be used to reduce transit time in stocking and can be applied to placing products in warehouses for utilizing space optimally.

Delivery Management

Reinforcement Learning is applied to solve the problem of split delivery vehicle routing. Q Learning is used to serve appropriate customers with one vehicle.

Finance Sector

Reinforcement Learning is being used for accounting, using trading strategies.

Why Is Reinforcement Learning Difficult?

One of the toughest parts of Reinforcement Learning is having to map the environment and include all possible moves. For example, consider a board game.

You have to apply artificial intelligence to what is learned. In theory, Reinforcement Learning should work perfectly because there are a lot of state jumps and complex moves in a board game. However, applying Reinforcement Learning by itself becomes difficult.

To get the best results, we apply a rule-based engine with Reinforcement Learning. If we don't apply a rule-based engine, there are so many options in board games that the agent will take forever to discover the path.

First of all, we apply simple rules so that the AI learns quickly and then, as the complexity increases, we apply Reinforcement Learning.

Figure 2-3 shows how applying Reinforcement Learning can be difficult.

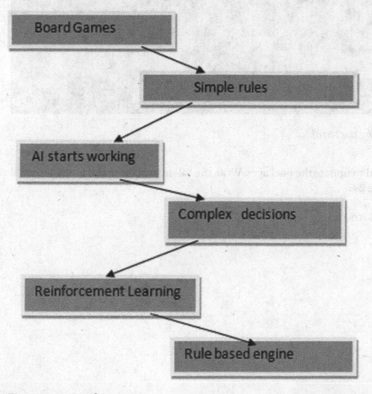

Figure 2-3. Reinforcement Learning with rules

Preparing the Machine

Before you can run the examples, you need to perform certain steps to install the software. The examples in this book use the Anaconda version of Python, so this section explains how to find and download it. First, you need to open a terminal. The process of starting the terminal is shown in Figure 2-4.

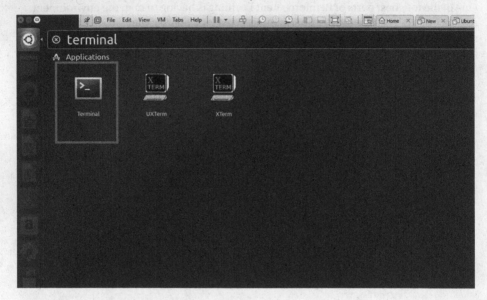

Figure 2-4. *Opening the terminal*

Next, you need to update the packages. Write the following command in the terminal to do so. See Figure 2-5.

```
sudo apt-get update
```

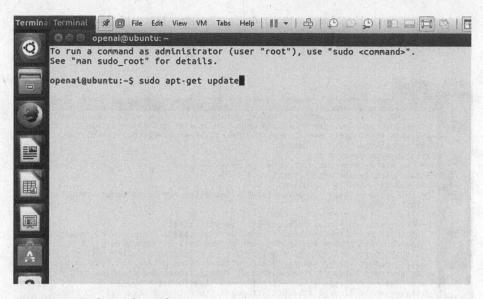

Figure 2-5. *Updating the packages*

After you run the update command, the required installation content is installed, as shown in Figure 2-6.

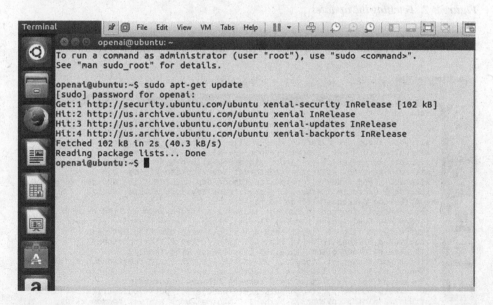

Figure 2-6. *Everything has been updated*

Now you can use another command for installing the required packages. Figure 2-7 shows the process.

sudo apt-get install golang python3-dev python-dev libcupti-dev libjpeg-
turbo8-dev make tmux htop chromium-browser git cmake zlib1g-dev libjpeg-dev
xvfb libav-tools xorg-dev python-opengl libboost-all-dev libsdl2-dev swig.

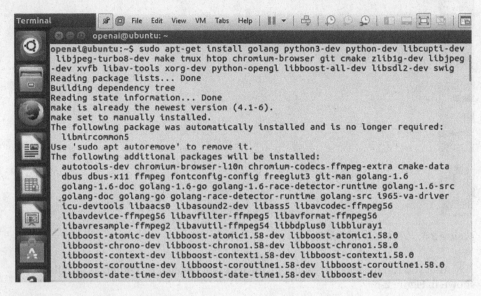

Figure 2-7. *Fetching the updates*

As shown in Figure 2-8, you'll need to type y and then press Enter to continue.

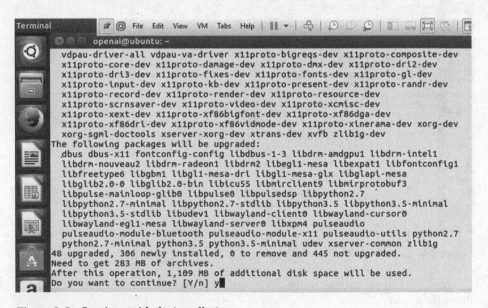

Figure 2-8. *Continue with the installation*

In the next step, the essential packages are downloaded and updated accordingly, as shown in Figure 2-9.

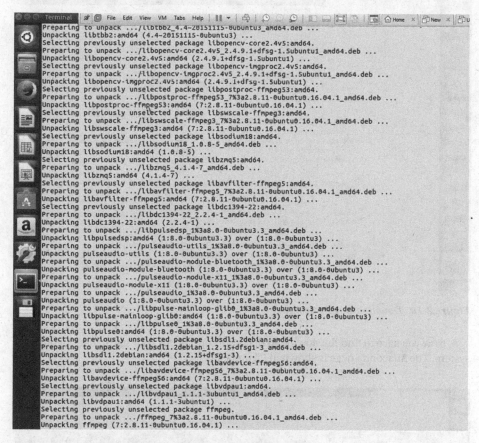

Figure 2-9. *Downloading and extracting the packages*

You have now installed the Anaconda distribution of Python. Next, you need to open a browser window for Ubuntu. This example shows Mozilla Firefox. Search for the Anaconda installation, as shown in Figure 2-10.

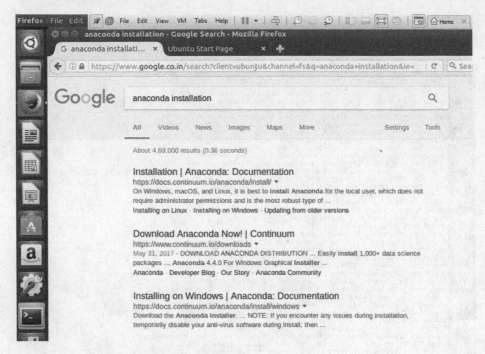

Figure 2-10. Downloading Anaconda

Now you have to find the download that's appropriate for your particular operating system. The Anaconda page is shown in Figure 2-11.

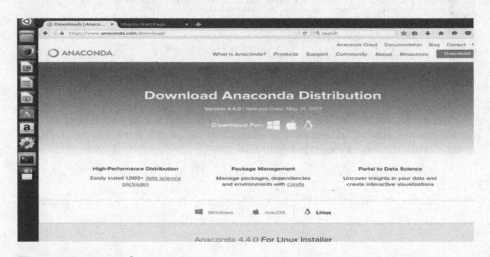

Figure 2-11. Anaconda page

Select the appropriate distribution of Anaconda, as shown in Figure 2-12.

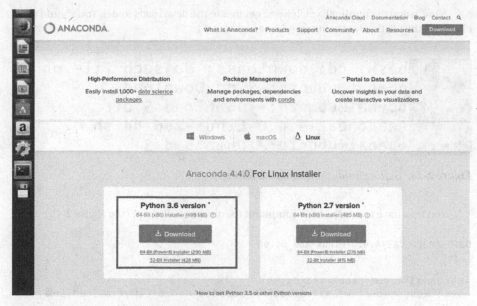

Figure 2-12. *Selecting the Anaconda version*

Save the file next, as shown in Figure 2-13.

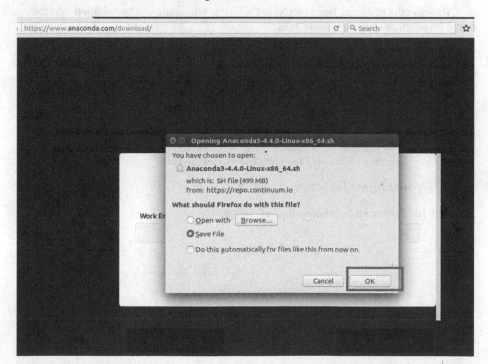

Figure 2-13. *Saving the file*

Now, using the terminal, you have to get inside the downloads folder. You should also check for the file that was being saved. See Figure 2-14.

Figure 2-14. *Getting inside the downloads folder*

You now have to use the bash command to run the shell script (see Figure 2-15):

```
bash Anaconda3-4.4.0-Linux-x86_64.sh
```

```
Anaconda3-4.4.0-Linux-x86_64.sh
openai@ubuntu:~/Downloads$ bash Anaconda3-4.4.0-Linux-x86 64.sh
```

Figure 2-15. *Running the shell script*

To select the platform, type yes and press Enter. Anaconda will be installed into the home location, as shown in Figure 2-16.

```
Please answer 'yes' or 'no':
>>> yes

Anaconda3 will now be installed into this location:
/home/openai/anaconda3

    - Press ENTER to confirm the location
    - Press CTRL-C to abort the installation
    - Or specify a different location below

[/home/openai/anaconda3] >>> 
```

Figure 2-16. *Setting up the Anaconda environment*

The next step, shown in Figure 2-17, will install all the important packages for Anaconda so that it is configured properly.

```
yes
installing: python-3.6.1-2 ...
installing: _license-1.1-py36_1 ...
installing: alabaster-0.7.10-py36_0 ...
installing: anaconda-client-1.6.3-py36_0 ...
installing: anaconda-navigator-1.6.2-py36_0 ...
installing: anaconda-project-0.6.0-py36_0 ...
installing: asn1crypto-0.22.0-py36_0 ...
installing: astroid-1.4.9-py36_0 ...
installing: astropy-1.3.2-np112py36_0 ...
installing: babel-2.4.0-py36_0 ...
installing: backports-1.0-py36_0 ...
installing: beautifulsoup4-4.6.0-py36_0 ...
installing: bitarray-0.8.1-py36_0 ...
installing: blaze-0.10.1-py36_0 ...
installing: bleach-1.5.0-py36_0 ...
installing: bokeh-0.12.5-py36_1 ...
installing: boto-2.46.1-py36_0 ...
installing: bottleneck-1.2.1-np112py36_0 ...
installing: cairo-1.14.8-0 ...
installing: cffi-1.10.0-py36_0 ...
installing: chardet-3.0.3-py36_0 ...
installing: click-6.7-py36_0 ...
installing: cloudpickle-0.2.2-py36_0 ...
installing: clyent-1.2.2-py36_0 ...
installing: colorama-0.3.9-py36_0 ...
installing: contextlib2-0.5.5-py36_0 ...
installing: cryptography-1.8.1-py36_0 ...
installing: curl-7.52.1-0 ...
installing: cycler-0.10.0-py36_0 ...
installing: cython-0.25.2-py36_0 ...
installing: cytoolz-0.8.2-py36_0 ...
installing: dask-0.14.3-py36_1 ...
installing: datashape-0.5.4-py36_0 ...
installing: dbus-1.10.10-0 ...
installing: decorator-4.0.11-py36_0 ...
installing: distributed-1.16.3-py36_0 ...
installing: docutils-0.13.1-py36_0 ...
installing: entrypoints-0.2.2-py36_1 ...
installing: et_xmlfile-1.0.1-py36_0 ...
installing: expat-2.1.0-0 ...
```

Figure 2-17. *Installing the key packages for Anaconda*

After the Anaconda installation is complete, you need to open a new terminal to set up your Anaconda environment. You have to create a new environment for Anaconda using the conda create command (see Figure 2-18).

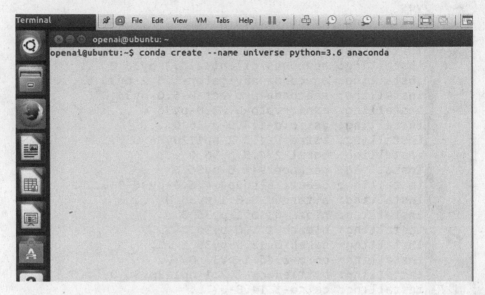

Figure 2-18. *Creating an environment*

This command keeps all the packages in an isolated place.

```
conda create --name universe python=3.6 anaconda
```

In the next step, the Anaconda environment will install the necessary packages. See Figure 2-19.

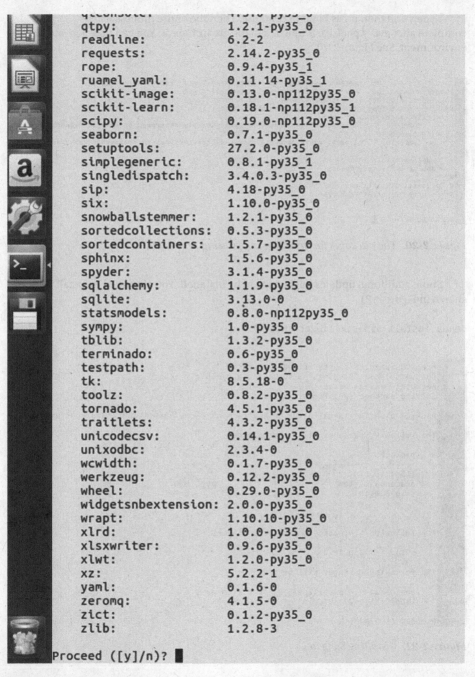

```
qtconsole:            4.3.0-py35_0
qtpy:                 1.2.1-py35_0
readline:             6.2-2
requests:             2.14.2-py35_0
rope:                 0.9.4-py35_1
ruamel_yaml:          0.11.14-py35_1
scikit-image:         0.13.0-np112py35_0
scikit-learn:         0.18.1-np112py35_1
scipy:                0.19.0-np112py35_0
seaborn:              0.7.1-py35_0
setuptools:           27.2.0-py35_0
simplegeneric:        0.8.1-py35_1
singledispatch:       3.4.0.3-py35_0
sip:                  4.18-py35_0
six:                  1.10.0-py35_0
snowballstemmer:      1.2.1-py35_0
sortedcollections:    0.5.3-py35_0
sortedcontainers:     1.5.7-py35_0
sphinx:               1.5.6-py35_0
spyder:               3.1.4-py35_0
sqlalchemy:           1.1.9-py35_0
sqlite:               3.13.0-0
statsmodels:          0.8.0-np112py35_0
sympy:                1.0-py35_0
tblib:                1.3.2-py35_0
terminado:            0.6-py35_0
testpath:             0.3-py35_0
tk:                   8.5.18-0
toolz:                0.8.2-py35_0
tornado:              4.5.1-py35_0
traitlets:            4.3.2-py35_0
unicodecsv:           0.14.1-py35_0
unixodbc:             2.3.4-0
wcwidth:              0.1.7-py35_0
werkzeug:             0.12.2-py35_0
wheel:                0.29.0-py35_0
widgetsnbextension:   2.0.0-py35_0
wrapt:                1.10.10-py35_0
xlrd:                 1.0.0-py35_0
xlsxwriter:           0.9.6-py35_0
xlwt:                 1.2.0-py35_0
xz:                   5.2.2-1
yaml:                 0.1.6-0
zeromq:               4.1.5-0
zict:                 0.1.2-py35_0
zlib:                 1.2.8-3

Proceed ([y]/n)?
```

Figure 2-19. *The packages for installing or updating Anaconda*

Type y and then press Enter to continue. Then the entire process will be complete after every package is updated in the environment. You can now activate the environment. See Figure 2-20.

```
spyder-3.1.4-p 100% |###############################| Time: 0:00:04 727.89 kB/s
widgetsnbexten 100% |###############################| Time: 0:00:00   1.67 MB/s
ipywidgets-6.0 100% |###############################| Time: 0:00:00 625.68 kB/s
anaconda-4.4.0 100% |###############################| Time: 0:00:00   7.77 kB/s
Extracting packages ...
[        COMPLETE        ]|###################################################################
Linking packages ...
[        COMPLETE        ]|###################################################################
#
# To activate this environment, use:
# > source activate universe
#
# To deactivate this environment, use:
# > source deactivate universe
#

openai@ubuntu:~$
```

Figure 2-20. *The packages for installing or updating Anaconda*

Some additional updates might need to be installed. You also need to install Swig, as shown in Figure 2-21.

```
conda install pip six libgcc swig
```

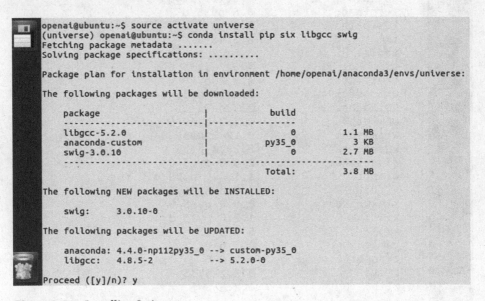

```
openai@ubuntu:~$ source activate universe
(universe) openai@ubuntu:~$ conda install pip six libgcc swig
Fetching package metadata .......
Solving package specifications: .........

Package plan for installation in environment /home/openai/anaconda3/envs/universe:

The following packages will be downloaded:

    package                    |            build
    ---------------------------|-----------------
    libgcc-5.2.0               |                0        1.1 MB
    anaconda-custom            |           py35_0        3 KB
    swig-3.0.10                |                0        2.7 MB
    ------------------------------------------------------------
                                           Total:        3.8 MB

The following NEW packages will be INSTALLED:

    swig:      3.0.10-0

The following packages will be UPDATED:

    anaconda: 4.4.0-np112py35_0 --> custom-py35_0
    libgcc:   4.8.5-2           --> 5.2.0-0

Proceed ([y]/n)? y
```

Figure 2-21. *Installing Swig too*

You will also have to install OpenCV in order to update certain packages, as shown in Figure 2-22.

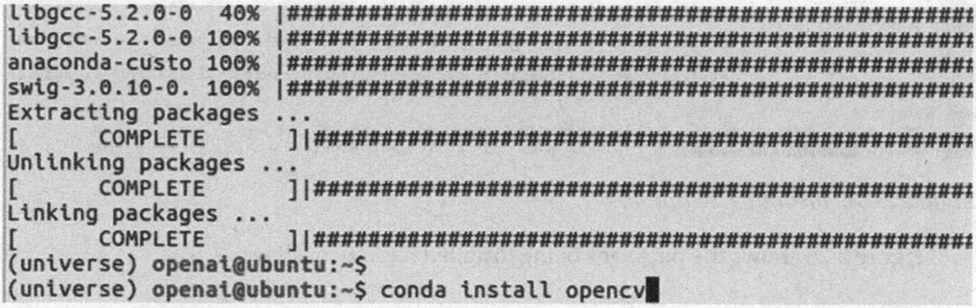

```
libgcc-5.2.0-0   40% |##################################################
libgcc-5.2.0-0  100% |##################################################
anaconda-custo  100% |##################################################
swig-3.0.10-0.  100% |##################################################
Extracting packages ...
[       COMPLETE       ]|##################################################
Unlinking packages ...
[       COMPLETE       ]|##################################################
Linking packages ...
[       COMPLETE       ]|##################################################
(universe) openai@ubuntu:~$
(universe) openai@ubuntu:~$ conda install opencv
```

Figure 2-22. *Installing OpenCV*

If there are updates to OpenCV, type y to install them too. See Figure 2-23.

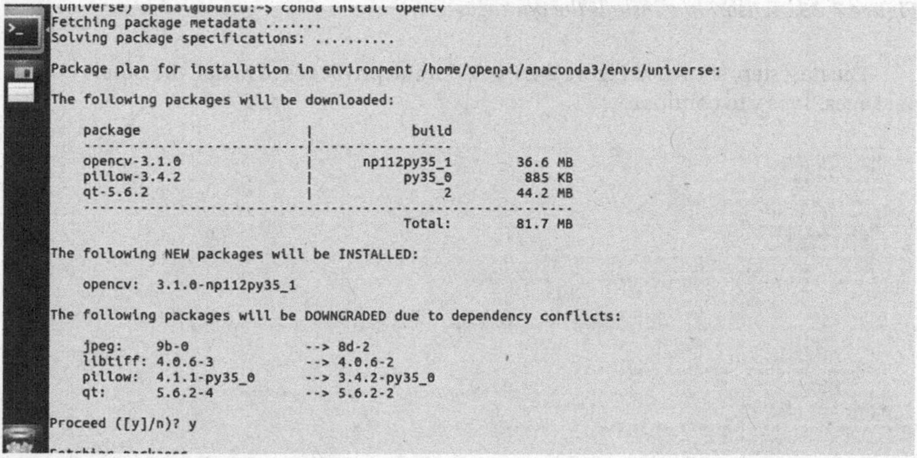

```
(universe) openai@ubuntu:~$ conda install opencv
Fetching package metadata .......
Solving package specifications: ..........

Package plan for installation in environment /home/openai/anaconda3/envs/universe:

The following packages will be downloaded:

    package                    |            build
    ---------------------------|-----------------
    opencv-3.1.0               |     np112py35_1         36.6 MB
    pillow-3.4.2               |          py35_0        885 KB
    qt-5.6.2                   |               2         44.2 MB
    ---------------------------------------------------
                                          Total:        81.7 MB

The following NEW packages will be INSTALLED:

    opencv:  3.1.0-np112py35_1

The following packages will be DOWNGRADED due to dependency conflicts:

    jpeg:    9b-0            --> 8d-2
    libtiff: 4.0.6-3         --> 4.0.6-2
    pillow:  4.1.1-py35_0    --> 3.4.2-py35_0
    qt:      5.6.2-4         --> 5.6.2-2

Proceed ([y]/n)? y
```

Figure 2-23. *Installing OpenCV*

Next, you need to install TensorFlow. This chapter shows how to install the CPU version. See Figure 2-24.

```
pip install --upgrade tensorflow
```

```
Fetching packages ...
opencv-3.1.0-n 100% |#####################################################
pillow-3.4.2-p 100% |#####################################################
qt-5.6.2-2.tar 100% |#####################################################
Extracting packages ...
[        COMPLETE        ]|#####################################################
Unlinking packages ...
[        COMPLETE        ]|#####################################################
Linking packages ...
[        COMPLETE        ]|#####################################################
(universe) openai@ubuntu:~$ pip install --upgrade tensorflow
Collecting tensorflow
  Downloading tensorflow-1.3.0-cp35-cp35m-manylinux1_x86_64.whl (43.1MB)
    61% |                              | 26.6MB 1.5MB/s eta 0:00:12
```

Figure 2-24. *Installing TensorFlow*

Figure 2-25 shows the packages being installed for TensorFlow.

```
FileNotFoundError: [Errno 2] No such file or directory: '/home/openai/anaconda3/envs/universe/lib/python3.5/site-packages/setuptools-27.2.0-py3.5.egg'
(universe) openai@ubuntu:~$ pip install --upgrade tensorflow
Requirement already up-to-date: tensorflow in ./anaconda3/envs/universe/lib/python3.5/site-packages
Requirement already up-to-date: six>=1.10.0 in ./anaconda3/envs/universe/lib/python3.5/site-packages (from tensorflow)
Requirement already up-to-date: protobuf>=3.3.0 in ./anaconda3/envs/universe/lib/python3.5/site-packages (from tensorflow)
Requirement already up-to-date: numpy>=1.11.0 in ./anaconda3/envs/universe/lib/python3.5/site-packages (from tensorflow)
Requirement already up-to-date: wheel>=0.26 in ./anaconda3/envs/universe/lib/python3.5/site-packages (from tensorflow)
Requirement already up-to-date: tensorflow-tensorboard<0.2.0,>=0.1.0 in ./anaconda3/envs/universe/lib/python3.5/site-packages (from tensorflow)
Requirement already up-to-date: setuptools in ./anaconda3/envs/universe/lib/python3.5/site-packages (from protobuf>=3.3.0->tensorflow)
Requirement already up-to-date: werkzeug>=0.11.10 in ./anaconda3/envs/universe/lib/python3.5/site-packages (from tensorflow-tensorboard<0.2.0,>=0.1.0->tensorflow)
Requirement already up-to-date: markdown>=2.6.8 in ./anaconda3/envs/universe/lib/python3.5/site-packages (from tensorflow-tensorboard<0.2.0,>=0.1.0->tensorflow)
Requirement already up-to-date: bleach==1.5.0 in ./anaconda3/envs/universe/lib/python3.5/site-packages (from tensorflow-tensorboard<0.2.0,>=0.1.0->tensorflow)
Requirement already up-to-date: html5lib==0.9999999 in ./anaconda3/envs/universe/lib/python3.5/site-packages (from tensorflow-tensorboard<0.2.0,>=0.1.0->tensorflow)
(universe) openai@ubuntu:~$
```

Figure 2-25. *TensorFlow installs the packages*

The next step, shown in Figure 2-26, asks for the privileges to install the other packages. Type y to continue.

```
(universe) openai@ubuntu:~$ sudo apt-get install \
>    apt-transport-https \
>    ca-certificates \
>    curl \
>    software-properties-common
[sudo] password for openai:
Reading package lists... Done
Building dependency tree
Reading state information... Done
ca-certificates is already the newest version (20160104ubuntu1).
ca-certificates set to manually installed.
The following package was automatically installed and is no longer required:
  libmircommon5
Use 'sudo apt autoremove' to remove it.
The following additional packages will be installed:
  libcairo-perl libcurl3-gnutls libglib-perl libgtk2-perl libpango-perl python3-software-properties software-properties-gtk
Suggested packages:
  libfont-freetype-perl libgtk2-perl-doc
The following NEW packages will be installed:
  libcairo-perl libglib-perl libgtk2-perl libpango-perl
The following packages will be upgraded:
  apt-transport-https curl libcurl3-gnutls python3-software-properties software-properties-common software-properties-gtk
6 upgraded, 4 newly installed, 0 to remove and 439 not upgraded.
Need to get 1,528 kB of archives.
After this operation, 4,815 kB of additional disk space will be used.
Do you want to continue? [Y/n]
```

Figure 2-26. *Package installation happens*

In the next section, we install Docker. We will first learn what Docker is.

Installing Docker

When you want to keep your containers in the cloud, Docker is the best option. Developers generally use Docker to minimize workloads on a single machine, because the entire architecture can be hosted on the developer environment. Enterprises use Docker to maintain an agile environment. Operators generally use Docker to keep an eye on apps and to run and manage them effectively.

Now you will install Docker, as it is essential for OpenAI Gym and Universe to work. You need to install Docker because, when you are training an environment, Docker is very responsive to simulations since it runs with low resources.

The command to be entered in the terminal is shown here:

```
$ sudo apt-get install \
    apt-transport-https \
    ca-certificates \
    curl \
    software-properties-common
```

The next command to enter is:

```
$ curl -fsSL https://download.docker.com/linux/ubuntu/gpg | sudo apt-key add
-
```

You use curl and the http link so that Docker can access these trusted key values. Now download the Docker type using this command:

```
$ sudo add-apt-repository \
    "deb [arch=amd64] https://download.docker.com/linux/ubuntu \
    $(lsb_release -cs) \
    stable"
```

Type this command to update Docker, as shown in Figure 2-27:

```
$ sudo apt-get update
```

```
UK
(universe) openai@ubuntu:~$ sudo add-apt-repository \
>    "deb [arch=amd64] https://download.docker.com/linux/ubuntu \
>    $(lsb_release -cs) \
>    stable"
(universe) openai@ubuntu:~$ sudo apt-get update
Get:1 http://security.ubuntu.com/ubuntu xenial-security InRelease [102 kB]
Hit:2 http://us.archive.ubuntu.com/ubuntu xenial InRelease
Get:3 http://us.archive.ubuntu.com/ubuntu xenial-updates InRelease [102 kB]
Get:4 https://download.docker.com/linux/ubuntu xenial InRelease [38.9 kB]
Get:5 https://download.docker.com/linux/ubuntu xenial/stable amd64 Packages [2,346 B]
Get:6 http://us.archive.ubuntu.com/ubuntu xenial-backports InRelease [102 kB]
Get:7 http://security.ubuntu.com/ubuntu xenial-security/main amd64 DEP-11 Metadata [60.1 kB]
Get:8 http://security.ubuntu.com/ubuntu xenial-security/main DEP-11 64x64 Icons [57.0 kB]
Get:9 http://security.ubuntu.com/ubuntu xenial-security/universe amd64 DEP-11 Metadata [48.7 kB]
Get:10 http://security.ubuntu.com/ubuntu xenial-security/universe DEP-11 64x64 Icons [69.1 kB]
Get:11 http://us.archive.ubuntu.com/ubuntu xenial-updates/main amd64 Packages [628 kB]
Get:12 http://us.archive.ubuntu.com/ubuntu xenial-updates/main i386 Packages [603 kB]
Get:13 http://us.archive.ubuntu.com/ubuntu xenial-updates/main Translation-en [259 kB]
Get:14 http://us.archive.ubuntu.com/ubuntu xenial-updates/main amd64 DEP-11 Metadata [305 kB]
Get:15 http://us.archive.ubuntu.com/ubuntu xenial-updates/main DEP-11 64x64 Icons [208 kB]
Get:16 http://us.archive.ubuntu.com/ubuntu xenial-updates/universe amd64 DEP-11 Metadata [171 kB]
Get:17 http://us.archive.ubuntu.com/ubuntu xenial-updates/universe DEP-11 64x64 Icons [226 kB]
Get:18 http://us.archive.ubuntu.com/ubuntu xenial-updates/multiverse amd64 DEP-11 Metadata [5,888 B]
Get:19 http://us.archive.ubuntu.com/ubuntu xenial-backports/main amd64 DEP-11 Metadata [3,328 B]
Get:20 http://us.archive.ubuntu.com/ubuntu xenial-backports/universe amd64 DEP-11 Metadata [5,136 B]
Fetched 2,997 kB in 12s (239 kB/s)
AppStream cache update completed, but some metadata was ignored due to errors.
```

Figure 2-27. *Updating the package*

Type this command to install Docker, as shown in Figure 2-28:

```
$ sudo apt-get install docker-ce
```

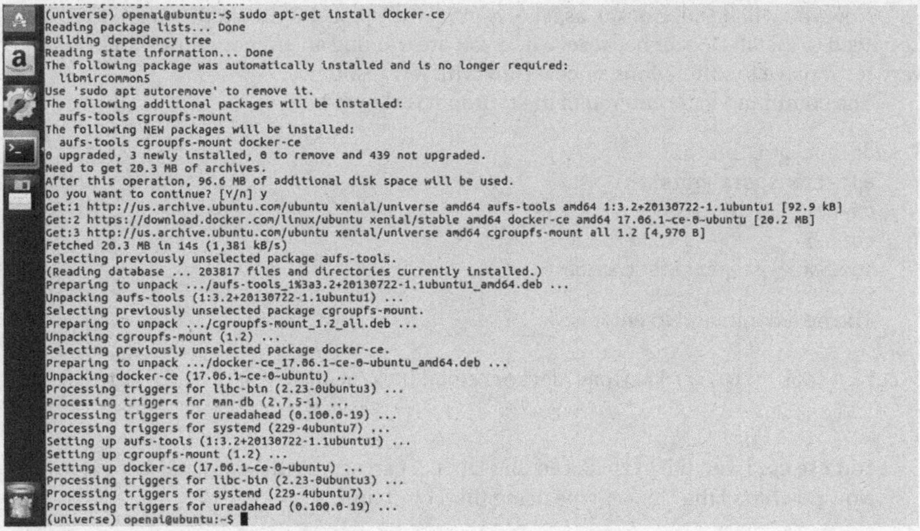

```
(universe) openai@ubuntu:~$ sudo apt-get install docker-ce
Reading package lists... Done
Building dependency tree
Reading state information... Done
The following package was automatically installed and is no longer required:
  libmircommon5
Use 'sudo apt autoremove' to remove it.
The following additional packages will be installed:
  aufs-tools cgroupfs-mount
The following NEW packages will be installed:
  aufs-tools cgroupfs-mount docker-ce
0 upgraded, 3 newly installed, 0 to remove and 439 not upgraded.
Need to get 20.3 MB of archives.
After this operation, 96.6 MB of additional disk space will be used.
Do you want to continue? [Y/n] y
Get:1 http://us.archive.ubuntu.com/ubuntu xenial/universe amd64 aufs-tools amd64 1:3.2+20130722-1.1ubuntu1 [92.9 kB]
Get:2 https://download.docker.com/linux/ubuntu xenial/stable amd64 docker-ce amd64 17.06.1-ce-0~ubuntu [20.2 MB]
Get:3 http://us.archive.ubuntu.com/ubuntu xenial/universe amd64 cgroupfs-mount all 1.2 [4,970 B]
Fetched 20.3 MB in 14s (1,381 kB/s)
Selecting previously unselected package aufs-tools.
(Reading database ... 203817 files and directories currently installed.)
Preparing to unpack .../aufs-tools_1%3a3.2+20130722-1.1ubuntu1_amd64.deb ...
Unpacking aufs-tools (1:3.2+20130722-1.1ubuntu1) ...
Selecting previously unselected package cgroupfs-mount.
Preparing to unpack .../cgroupfs-mount_1.2_all.deb ...
Unpacking cgroupfs-mount (1.2) ...
Selecting previously unselected package docker-ce.
Preparing to unpack .../docker-ce_17.06.1-ce-0~ubuntu_amd64.deb ...
Unpacking docker-ce (17.06.1-ce-0~ubuntu) ...
Processing triggers for libc-bin (2.23-0ubuntu3) ...
Processing triggers for man-db (2.7.5-1) ...
Processing triggers for ureadahead (0.100.0-19) ...
Processing triggers for systemd (229-4ubuntu7) ...
Setting up aufs-tools (1:3.2+20130722-1.1ubuntu1) ...
Setting up cgroupfs-mount (1.2) ...
Setting up docker-ce (17.06.1-ce-0~ubuntu) ...
Processing triggers for libc-bin (2.23-0ubuntu3) ...
Processing triggers for systemd (229-4ubuntu7) ...
Processing triggers for ureadahead (0.100.0-19) ...
(universe) openai@ubuntu:~$ █
```

Figure 2-28. *Docker installation*

To test Docker, use this command (see Figure 2-29):

```
$ sudo service docker start
$ sudo docker run hello-world
```

```
(universe) openai@ubuntu:~$ sudo service docker start
(universe) openai@ubuntu:~$ sudo docker run hello-world
Unable to find image 'hello-world:latest' locally
latest: Pulling from library/hello-world
b04784fba78d: Pull complete
Digest: sha256:f3b3b28a45160805bb16542c9531888519430e9e6d6ffc09d72261b0d26ff74f
Status: Downloaded newer image for hello-world:latest

Hello from Docker!
This message shows that your installation appears to be working correctly.

To generate this message, Docker took the following steps:
 1. The Docker client contacted the Docker daemon.
 2. The Docker daemon pulled the "hello-world" image from the Docker Hub.
 3. The Docker daemon created a new container from that image which runs the
    executable that produces the output you are currently reading.
 4. The Docker daemon streamed that output to the Docker client, which sent it
    to your terminal.

To try something more ambitious, you can run an Ubuntu container with:
 $ docker run -it ubuntu bash

Share images, automate workflows, and more with a free Docker ID:
 https://cloud.docker.com/

For more examples and ideas, visit:
 https://docs.docker.com/engine/userguide/

(universe) openai@ubuntu:~$ █
```

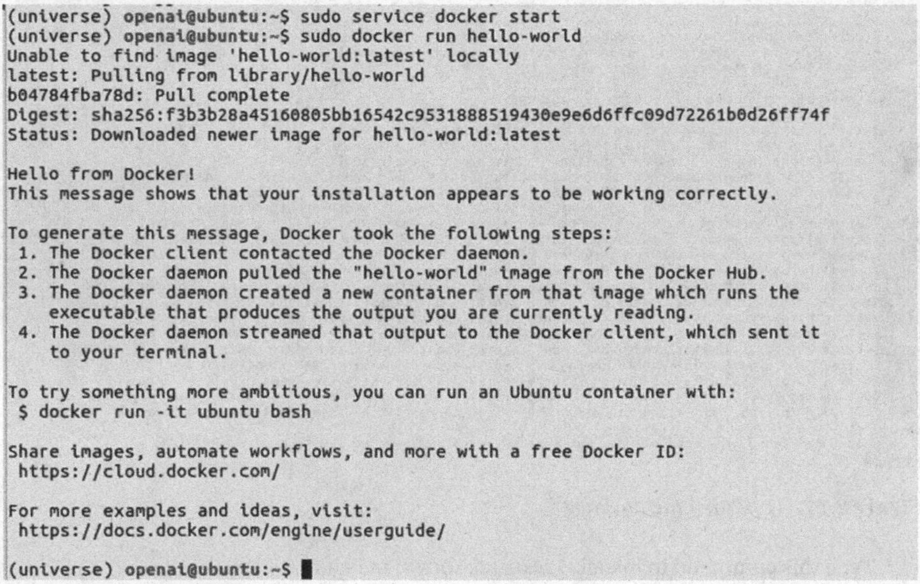

Figure 2-29. *Testing docker*

An Example of Reinforcement Learning with Python

This section goes through an example of Reinforcement Learning and explains the flow of the algorithm. You'll see how Reinforcement Learning can be applied. This section uses an open source GitHub repo that has a very good example of Reinforcement Learning. You will need to clone it to work with it.

The GitHub repo link is https://github.com/MorvanZhou/Reinforcement-learning-with-tensorflow. Within the Ubuntu module, get inside the terminal and start cloning the repo, as shown in Figure 2-30.

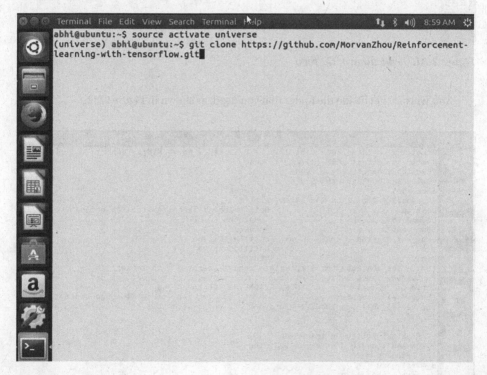

Figure 2-30. *Cloning the repo*

Figure 2-31 shows how the repo is replicated.

Figure 2-31. *Replication of the repo*

You will next get inside the folder that you used, as shown in Figure 2-32.

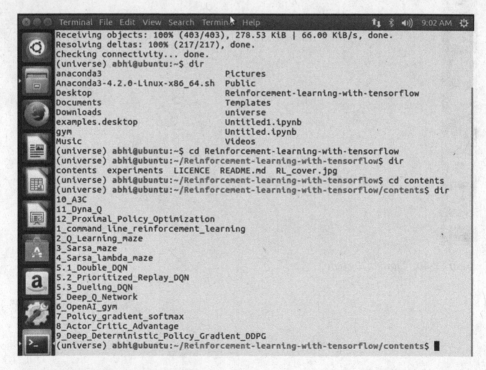

Figure 2-32. *Getting inside the folder*

We are working with a scenario of Reinforcement Learning where we are applying the letter O as a wanderer. That wanderer wants to get the treasure T as fast as it can.

The condition looks like this:

```
O-----T
```

The wanderer tries to find the quickest path to reach the treasure. During each episode, the steps the wanderer takes to reach the treasure are counted. With each episode, the condition improves and the number of steps declines.

Here are some of the basic steps in terms of Reinforcement Learning:

- The program tries to work with actions, as actions are very important in terms of Reinforcement Learning.

- The available actions for this wanderer is moving left or right:

```
ACTIONS = ['left','right']
```

- The wanderer can be considered the agent.

- The number of states (also called the number of steps) is limited to 6 in this example:

```
N_States = 6;
```

Now you need to apply hyperparameters for Reinforcement Learning.

What Are Hyperparameters?

Hyperparameters are variables that were set before setting the model's parameters. Generally, they are different from the parameters of the model for the underlying system under analysis.

We introduce epsilon, alpha, and gamma.

- Epsilon is the greedy factor
- Alpha is the learning rate
- Gamma is the discount factor

The maximum number of episodes in this case is 13. The refresh rate is when the scenario is refreshed.

Writing the Code

To create the process from which the computer learns, we have to formulate a table. This process is known as Q Learning and the table is called a Q table (You will learn more about Q Learning in the next chapter.) All the key elements are stored in the Q table and all the decisions are made based on the Q table.

```
def build_q_table(n_states, actions):
    table = pd.DataFrame(
        np.zeros((n_states, len(actions))),      # q_table initial values
        columns=actions,    # actions's name
    )
    # print(table)     # show table
    return table
```

Now we have to take actions. To do so, we use this code:

```
def choose_action(state, q_table):
    # This is how to choose an action
    state_actions = q_table.iloc[state, :]
    if (np.random.uniform() > EPSILON) or (state_actions.all() == 0):  # act
    non-greedy or state-action have no value
        action_name = np.random.choice(ACTIONS)
    else:    # act greedy
        action_name = state_actions.argmax()
    return action_name
```

Now we create the environment and determine how the agents will work within the environment:

```
def get_env_feedback(S, A):
    # This is how the agent will interact with the environment
    if A == 'right':     # move right
        if S == N_STATES - 2:   # terminate
            S_ = 'terminal'
            R = 1
        else:
            S_ = S + 1
            R = 0
    else:   # move left
        R = 0
        if S == 0:
            S_ = S  # reach the wall
        else:
            S_ = S - 1
    return S_, R
```

This function prints the wanderer and treasure hunt conditions:

```
def update_env(S, episode, step_counter):
    # This is how the environment be updated
    env_list = ['-']*(N_STATES-1) + ['T']   # '---------T' our environment
    if S == 'terminal':
        interaction = 'Episode %s: total_steps = %s' % (episode+1, step_
        counter)
```

```
        print('\r{}'.format(interaction), end='')
        time.sleep(2)
        print('\r                                      ', end='')
    else:
        env_list[S] = 'o'
        interaction = ''.join(env_list)
        print('\r{}'.format(interaction), end='')
        time.sleep(FRESH_TIME)
```

The rl() method calls the Q Learning scenario, which we discuss in next chapter:

```
def rl():
    # main part of RL loop
    q_table = build_q_table(N_STATES, ACTIONS)
    for episode in range(MAX_EPISODES):
        step_counter = 0
        S = 0
        is_terminated = False
        update_env(S, episode, step_counter)
        while not is_terminated:

            A = choose_action(S, q_table)
            S_, R = get_env_feedback(S, A)  # take action & get next state
            and reward
            q_predict = q_table.ix[S, A]
            if S_ != 'terminal':
                q_target = R + GAMMA * q_table.iloc[S_, :].max()   # next
                state is not terminal
            else:
                q_target = R      # next state is terminal
                is_terminated = True    # terminate this episode

            q_table.ix[S, A] += ALPHA * (q_target - q_predict)  # update
            S = S_  # move to next state

            update_env(S, episode, step_counter+1)
            step_counter += 1
    return q_table

if __name__ == "__main__":
    q_table = rl()
    print('\r\nQ-table:\n')
    print(q_table)
```

The full code looks like this:

```python
import numpy as np
import pandas as pd
import time

np.random.seed(2)  # reproducible

N_STATES = 6   # the length of the 1 dimensional world
ACTIONS = ['left', 'right']     # available actions
EPSILON = 0.9   # greedy police
ALPHA = 0.1      # learning rate
GAMMA = 0.9     # discount factor
MAX_EPISODES = 13   # maximum episodes
FRESH_TIME = 0.3    # fresh time for one move

def build_q_table(n_states, actions):
    table = pd.DataFrame(
        np.zeros((n_states, len(actions))),      # q_table initial values
        columns=actions,     # actions's name
    )
    # print(table)    # show table
    return table

def choose_action(state, q_table):
    # This is how to choose an action
    state_actions = q_table.iloc[state, :]
    if (np.random.uniform() > EPSILON) or (state_actions.all() == 0):  # act
non-greedy or state-action have no value
        action_name = np.random.choice(ACTIONS)
    else:   # act greedy
        action_name = state_actions.argmax()
    return action_name

def get_env_feedback(S, A):
    # This is how agent will interact with the environment
    if A == 'right':     # move right
        if S == N_STATES - 2:   # terminate
            S_ = 'terminal'
            R = 1
        else:
            S_ = S + 1
            R = 0
    else:   # move left
        R = 0
        if S == 0:
            S_ = S   # reach the wall
        else:
```

```python
            S_ = S - 1
        return S_, R

def update_env(S, episode, step_counter):
    # This is how environment be updated
    env_list = ['-']*(N_STATES-1) + ['T']   # '---------T' our environment
    if S == 'terminal':
        interaction = 'Episode %s: total_steps = %s' % (episode+1, step_
        counter)
        print('\r{}'.format(interaction), end='')
        time.sleep(2)
        print('\r                                    ', end='')
    else:
        env_list[S] = 'o'
        interaction = ''.join(env_list)
        print('\r{}'.format(interaction), end='')
        time.sleep(FRESH_TIME)

def rl():
    # main part of RL loop
    q_table = build_q_table(N_STATES, ACTIONS)
    for episode in range(MAX_EPISODES):
        step_counter = 0
        S = 0
        is_terminated = False
        update_env(S, episode, step_counter)
        while not is_terminated:

            A = choose_action(S, q_table)
            S_, R = get_env_feedback(S, A)  # take action & get next state
            and reward
            q_predict = q_table.ix[S, A]
            if S_ != 'terminal':
                q_target = R + GAMMA * q_table.iloc[S_, :].max()   # next
                state is not terminal
            else:
                q_target = R     # next state is terminal
                is_terminated = True    # terminate this episode

            q_table.ix[S, A] += ALPHA * (q_target - q_predict)  # update
            S = S_  # move to next state

            update_env(S, episode, step_counter+1)
            step_counter += 1
    return q_table

if __name__ == "__main__":
    q_table = rl()
    print('\r\nQ-table:\n')
    print(q_table)
```

Let's now run the program and analyze the output. You need to get inside the cloned GitHub repo and into the required folder, as shown in Figure 2-33.

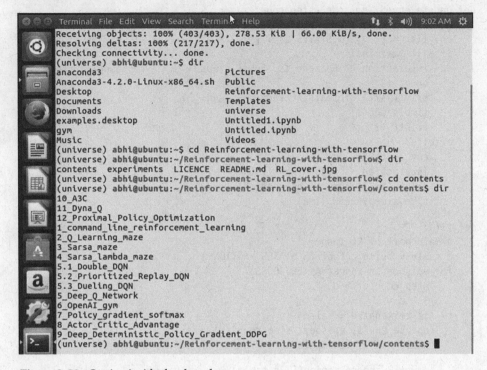

Figure 2-33. *Getting inside the cloned repo*

Now you need to get inside the directory to run the program, as shown in Figure 2-34.

```
(universe) abhi@ubuntu:~/Reinforcement-learning-with-tensorflow/contents/1_comma
nd_line_reinforcement_learning$ dir
treasure_on_right.py
(universe) abhi@ubuntu:~/Reinforcement-learning-with-tensorflow/contents/1_comma
nd_line_reinforcement_learning$
```

Figure 2-34. *Checking the directory*

Now you have to run the program called `treasure_on_right.py`, which places the treasure to the right of the agent. See Figure 2-35.

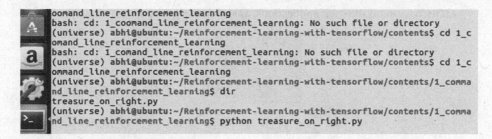

```
oomand_line_reinforcement_learning
bash: cd: 1_coomand_line_reinforcement_learning: No such file or directory
(universe) abhi@ubuntu:~/Reinforcement-learning-with-tensorflow/contents$ cd 1_c
omand_line_reinforcement_learning
bash: cd: 1_comand_line_reinforcement_learning: No such file or directory
(universe) abhi@ubuntu:~/Reinforcement-learning-with-tensorflow/contents$ cd 1_c
ommand_line_reinforcement_learning
(universe) abhi@ubuntu:~/Reinforcement-learning-with-tensorflow/contents/1_comma
nd_line_reinforcement_learning$ dir
treasure_on_right.py
(universe) abhi@ubuntu:~/Reinforcement-learning-with-tensorflow/contents/1_comma
nd_line_reinforcement_learning$ python treasure_on_right.py
```

Figure 2-35. *Running the Python file*

The program is running iterations, as shown in Figure 2-36.

```
treasure_on_right.py
(universe) abhi@ubuntu:~/Reinforcement-learning-with-tensorflow/contents/1_comma
nd_line_reinforcement_learning$ python treasure_on_right.py
--o--T
```

Figure 2-36. *As the iteration happens*

As the program and the simulation complete, the final result is interpreted as a Q table, where on each step of completing the cycle, the values reflect how much time it spent in the left and right directions. Figure 2-37 shows the completed Q table.

```
Q-table:

        left       right
0    0.000001    0.005728
1    0.000271    0.032612
2    0.002454    0.111724
3    0.000073    0.343331
4    0.000810    0.745813
5    0.000000    0.000000
```

Figure 2-37. *The Q table created as a result*

What Is MDP?

MDP (Markov Decision Process) is a framework that involves creating mathematical formulas and models for decision making where part of it is random and part of it remains in the hands of a decision maker.

MDPs have many different applications, as shown in Figure 2-38.

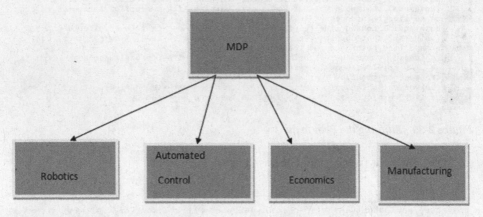

Figure 2-38. *MDP and its applications*

Every state in MDP satisfies the Markov property.

The Markov Property

In the world of Reinforcement Learning, the Markov property refers to a memory-less property that is stochastic. *Stochastic* means a general mathematical object consisting of random variables. When we are not storing a value of a variable because in each iteration there is a change, we call it stochastic. See Figure 2-39.

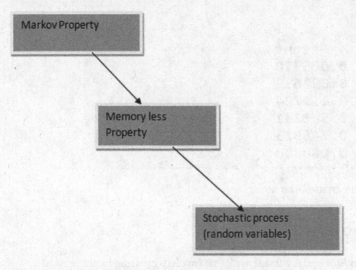

Figure 2-39. *The Markov property process*

We talk about the Markov Chain in the next section.

The Markov Chain

If a mathematical property has either a discrete state space or a discrete index set, it is known as a Markov Chain. The Markov Chain works in two ways, as shown in Figure 2-40.

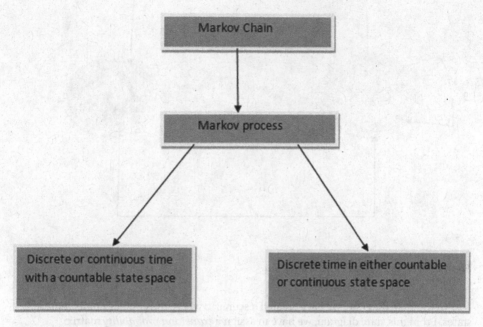

Figure 2-40. *Markov Chain*

Let's look at Markov Chains using an example. This example compares sales of Rin detergent versus the other detergents in the market. Assume that sales of Rin is 20 percent of the total detergent sales, which means the rest comprise 80 percent. People who use Rin detergent are defined as A; the others are A'.

Now we define a rule. Of the people who use Rin detergent, 90% of them continue to use it after a week whereas 10% shift to another brand.

Similarly, 70% of the people who use another detergent shift to Rin after a week, and the rest continue to use the other detergent.

To analyze these conditions, we need a state diagram. See Figure 2-41.

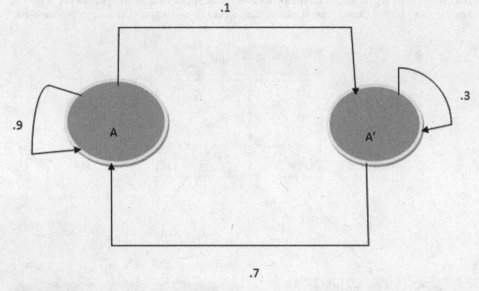

Figure 2-41. *Rin detergent state diagram*

In the state diagram, we have created a scenario where the circular points represent states. From this state diagram, we have to assign a *transition probability* matrix.

The transition probability matrix we get from the state diagram is shown in Figure 2-42.

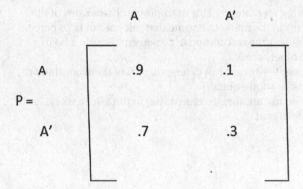

Figure 2-42. *The transition probability matrix*

To determine the use of Rin after two weeks, we have to apply a principle. This principle is common for each and every process you try.

It can be shown as a line connection, as shown in Figure 2-43.

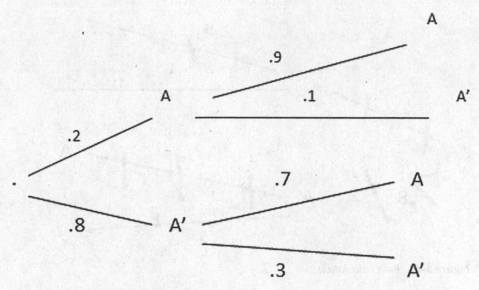

Figure 2-43. *A connected graph*

From the origin, we have two paths—one for Rin detergent (through A) and the other for the rest (that is A′). Here is how the path is created.

1. From the origin, we create a path for A, so we have to focus on the transition probability matrix.

2. We trace the path of A.

3. From the starting market share, the detergent Rin has a market value of 20%.

4. From the starting point A, we focus on the transition probability matrix.

There is a 90% probability of staying on A, so the other 10% change to the alternate path (to A′).

Figure 2-44 shows this path calculation graphically.

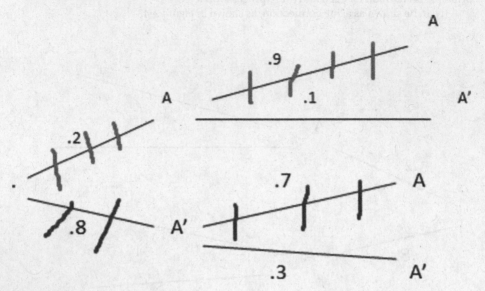

Figure 2-44. *Path calculation*

The total path probability is determined as so: P = .2 *.9 + .8*.7 = .18 + .56 = .74. This is the percentage of people using Rin after one week.

This formula can also be conceptualized as the current market share (SO) and transition probability (P):

SO * P = market share after one week
See Figure 2-45.

$S_0 \cdot P =$

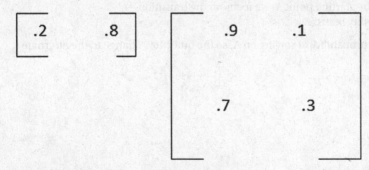

Figure 2-45. *The matrix created for the next week*

The calculation is .2 * .9 + .8*.7 = .74
.2*.1 + .8*.3 =.26
[.74 .26] = S1

Let's work on a first state matrix. After one week, the sale of Rin detergent is 74% of the market. The other brands then make up 26% of the market.

Now try to find the percentage of people using Rin detergent after two weeks. Figure 2-46 shows the calculation that we need to do after two weeks.

$S_1.P$

=

			A	A'
.74	.26	A	.9	.1
		A'	.7	.3

Figure 2-46. *The next transition matrix*

So the result is:

A A'
= [.848 .152]

After two weeks, 84.8% of the people will use Rin and 15.2% will use other detergents.

One question you might have is whether the sale of Rin will ever maximize to 100% of the market. As we go along, the matrix will become stationary after a certain number of iterations and finally settle at:

A A'
= [.75 .25]

After going through the basics of the Markov state and the Markov Chain, it's time to focus on MDPs again.

MDPs

Almost all Reinforcement Learning problems can be formalized as MDPs. MDPs create a condition that's prevalent for applying Reinforcement Learning. The essentials of MDPs are a continued Markov process.

A state (St) is Markov if and only if it meets the criteria shown in Figure 2-47.

$$P[\,S_{t+1}\,|\,S_t\,] \quad = \quad P[\,S_{t+1}\,|\,S_{1,\ldots\ldots},S_t]$$

Figure 2-47. *The Markov state property*

The state captures all relevant information from the history. We do not have to retain everything in history because only the previous state determines what will happen now.

For a Markov state (s) and successor state (s'), the state transition probability is defined in Figure 2-48.

$$P_{ss'} = P[\,S_{t+1} = S' \mid S_{t=s}]$$

$$P = \begin{bmatrix} & P_{11}\ldots\ldots\ldots\ldots\ldots\ldots\ldots P_{1n} & \end{bmatrix}$$

Figure 2-48. *The transitive probability*

MDP is a Markov reward process with a decision factor in it. It is a type of environment where all the states are Markov.

An MDP is a five tuple < S, A, P, R, Gamma>:

- S stands for state

- A stands for action

- P is a policy

- R stands for reward

Policy (π) is a distribution over actions in a given state. A policy is a function or a decision-making process that allows transitions from one state to another.

SARSA

SARSA stands for State Action Reward next State and next Action. It is a different kind of Reinforcement Learning approach and is generally derived from temporal difference learning. We'll discuss temporal difference learning first.

Temporal Difference Learning

This type of learning is based on its own vicinity or its own range. We generally apply temporal difference learning when we are in a state and want to know what is happening in successive states.

The general idea is that we want to predict the best path over a period of time.

We go from state S0 to state SF. We get rewards in each state. We will be trying to predict the discounted sum of rewards. See Figure 2-49.

$$S_0 \xrightarrow{\quad r_0 \quad} S_1 \xrightarrow{\quad r_1 \quad} S_2 \xrightarrow{\quad r_2 \quad} S_F$$

Figure 2-49. *State transition*

We start by looking at the Markov Chain, as shown in Figure 2-50.

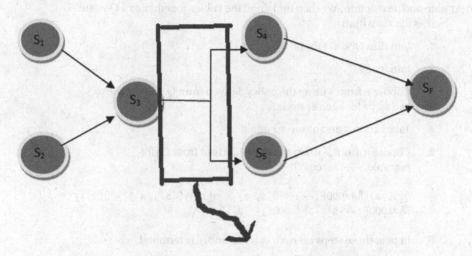

Stochastic Transition

Figure 2-50. *The Markov Chain*

The equation states that the value function maps the state to some number. This number is set to 0 if it is in the final state (see Figure 2-51).

$$V(s) = \begin{cases} 0, & \text{if } S = S_F \\ E[r + \gamma\, v(s')], & \text{otherwise} \end{cases}$$

Figure 2-51. *The value function*

For any state, the value is the expected value of the reward (r) and the discounted value of the ending state.

How SARSA Works

Now we get into SARSA. SARSA is known as an own policy Reinforcement Learning. An own policy means that we can see only our own experiences.

It accumulates updates in one or more steps and learns to update from its experiences.

From the current state, we choose an action and then get to the next state. At the next state, we choose another state and use the current state and the current action with the next state and next action. We then update all the values together as a Q value.

Here is the algorithm:

1. Initialize Q(s, a) arbitrarily.

2. Initialize s.

3. Choose a from s using the policy derived from Q. Repeat these two steps for each episode.

4. Take action a and observe r and s'.

5. Choose a' from s' using the policy derived from Q (for example, ----E-greedy).

    ```
    Q(s, a) &#x00DF;----- Q(s, a) + α[r +γQ(s', a') - Q(s,a)]
    S&#x00DF;---s'; a&#x00DF;-- a';
    ```

6. Repeat these steps for each episode until s is terminal.

Q Learning

Q Learning is a model-free Reinforcement Learning technique. Figure 2-52 illustrates the general procedure for Q Learning.

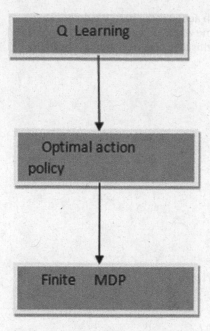

Figure 2-52. *The Q Learning process*

What Is Q?

Q can be stated as a function that consists of two parameters—s and a. The a parameter can also be referred to as a table.

Q represents the value that an action a takes with state s.

```
Q[s, a] = Immediate reward + discounted reward
```

The immediate reward is the point given when the agent moves from one state to another while doing an action.

The discounted reward is the point given for future references.

How to Use Q

We generally come up with scenarios where we have to find out where we can utilize the Q table values or the Q value so Q is implemented in this process.

We are looking at what action to take or which policy to implement when we are in state s. We use the Q table to get the best result.

If we are in state s, we need to determine which action is the best. We do not change s, but we go through all the values of a and determine which one is the largest. That will be the action we should take. Mathematically, this idea is represented as shown in Figures 2-53 and 2-54.

$$\Pi(s) = \text{argmax}_a (Q[s, a])$$

Figure 2-53. *The policy equation*

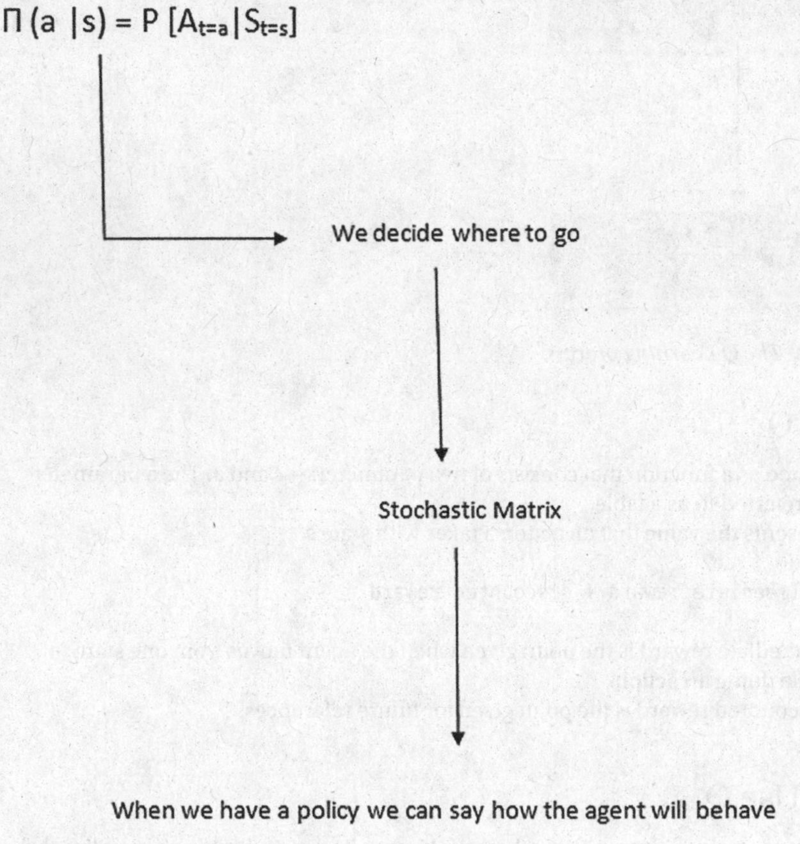

$$\Pi (a \mid s) = P [A_{t=a} \mid S_{t=s}]$$

We decide where to go

Stochastic Matrix

When we have a policy we can say how the agent will behave

Figure 2-54. *How policy works*

For MDP, the policy we should implement depends on the current state. We maximize the rewards to get the optimal solution.

SARSA Implementation in Python

Recall that SARSA is as self policy Reinforcement Learning approach.

For example, SARSA can be used to solve a maze. Using the SARSA approach, we cannot compare two different maze environments. We have to stick to one maze and we'll use the previous as an example. Also, we cannot compare this maze with another outside maze; we have to stick to the maze that we are working on.

The best thing about SARSA is that it can learn from the current state compared to the next state or to subsequent states. We accumulate all the experiences and learn from them.

Let's break this idea down more. This scenario states that the update can be done on a Q table by comparing the changes in subsequent steps and then making a decision. This idea is illustrated in Figure 2-55.

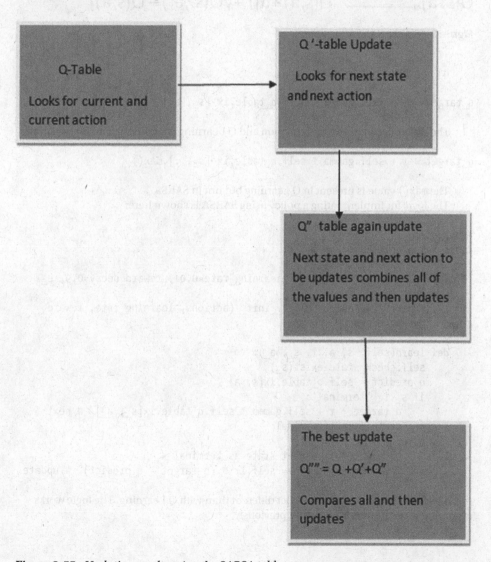

Q-Table

Looks for current and current action

Q'-table Update

Looks for next state and next action

Q'' table again update

Next state and next action to be updates combines all of the values and then updates

The best update

Q'''' = Q +Q'+Q''

Compares all and then updates

Figure 2-55. *Updating results using the SARSA table*

The learning method in Python is different for SARSA. It looks like this:

```
def learn(self, s, a, r, s_, a_)
```

This method depends on the state, the action, the reward, the next state, and the next action.

If we compare the algorithm and convert it to Python, the construct for this equation is shown in Figure 2-56.

$$Q(s, a) \longleftarrow Q(s,a) + \alpha[r + \gamma Q(s',a') - Q(s,a)]$$

Figure 2-56. *The SARSA equation*

It's converted to the following:

```
q_target = r + self.gamma * self.q_table.ix [s_, a_]
```

The difference between this equation and Q Learning is the change in this equation:

```
q_target = r + self.gamma * self.q_table.ix [s_, :].max()
```

The max() value is present in Q Learning but not in SARSA.

The logic for implementing a policy using SARSA is shown here:

```
# on-policy
class SarsaTable(RL):

    def __init__(self, actions, learning_rate=0.01, reward_decay=0.9, e_
    greedy=0.9):
        super(SarsaTable, self).__init__(actions, learning_rate, reward_
        decay, e_greedy)

    def learn(self, s, a, r, s_, a_):
        self.check_state_exist(s_)
        q_predict = self.q_table.ix[s, a]
        if s_ != 'terminal':
            q_target = r + self.gamma * self.q_table.ix[s_, a_]  # next
            state is not terminal
        else:
            q_target = r  # next state is terminal
        self.q_table.ix[s, a] += self.lr * (q_target - q_predict)  # update
```

The learning process is somewhat different than with Q Learning. The logic works according to the principle discussed previously.

We combine the state and action of the current status with the next state and next action. This in turn updates the Q table. This is the way the learning works.

```python
def update():
    for episode in range(100):
        # initial observation
        observation = env.reset()

        # RL choose action based on observation
        action = RL.choose_action(str(observation))

        while True:
            # fresh env
            env.render()

            # RL take action and get next observation and reward
            observation_, reward, done = env.step(action)

            # RL choose action based on next observation
            action_ = RL.choose_action(str(observation_))

            # RL learn from this transition (s, a, r, s, a) ==> Sarsa
            RL.learn(str(observation), action, reward, str(observation_),
            action_)

            # swap observation and action
            observation = observation_
            action = action_

            # break while loop when end of this episode
            if done:
                break
```

Here is the code for creating the maze:

```python
import numpy as np
import time
import sys
if sys.version_info.major == 2:
    import Tkinter as tk
else:
    import tkinter as tk

UNIT = 40    # pixels
MAZE_H = 4   # grid height
MAZE_W = 4   # grid width
```

```python
class Maze(tk.Tk, object):
    def __init__(self):
        super(Maze, self).__init__()
        self.action_space = ['u', 'd', 'l', 'r']
        self.n_actions = len(self.action_space)
        self.title('maze')
        self.geometry('{0}x{1}'.format(MAZE_H * UNIT, MAZE_H * UNIT))
        self._build_maze()

    def _build_maze(self):
        self.canvas = tk.Canvas(self, bg='white',
                                height=MAZE_H * UNIT,
                                width=MAZE_W * UNIT)

        # create grids
        for c in range(0, MAZE_W * UNIT, UNIT):
            x0, y0, x1, y1 = c, 0, c, MAZE_H * UNIT
            self.canvas.create_line(x0, y0, x1, y1)
        for r in range(0, MAZE_H * UNIT, UNIT):
            x0, y0, x1, y1 = 0, r, MAZE_H * UNIT, r
            self.canvas.create_line(x0, y0, x1, y1)

        # create origin
        origin = np.array([20, 20])

        # hell
        hell1_center = origin + np.array([UNIT * 2, UNIT])
        self.hell1 = self.canvas.create_rectangle(
            hell1_center[0] - 15, hell1_center[1] - 15,
            hell1_center[0] + 15, hell1_center[1] + 15,
            fill='black')
        # hell
        hell2_center = origin + np.array([UNIT, UNIT * 2])
        self.hell2 = self.canvas.create_rectangle(
            hell2_center[0] - 15, hell2_center[1] - 15,
            hell2_center[0] + 15, hell2_center[1] + 15,
            fill='black')

        # create oval
        oval_center = origin + UNIT * 2
        self.oval = self.canvas.create_oval(
            oval_center[0] - 15, oval_center[1] - 15,
            oval_center[0] + 15, oval_center[1] + 15,
            fill='yellow')
```

```python
    # create red rect
    self.rect = self.canvas.create_rectangle(
        origin[0] - 15, origin[1] - 15,
        origin[0] + 15, origin[1] + 15,
        fill='red')

    # pack all
    self.canvas.pack()

def reset(self):
    self.update()
    time.sleep(0.5)
    self.canvas.delete(self.rect)
    origin = np.array([20, 20])
    self.rect = self.canvas.create_rectangle(
        origin[0] - 15, origin[1] - 15,
        origin[0] + 15, origin[1] + 15,
        fill='red')
    # return observation
    return self.canvas.coords(self.rect)

def step(self, action):
    s = self.canvas.coords(self.rect)
    base_action = np.array([0, 0])
    if action == 0:    # up
        if s[1] > UNIT:
            base_action[1] -= UNIT
    elif action == 1:    # down
        if s[1] < (MAZE_H - 1) * UNIT:
            base_action[1] += UNIT
    elif action == 2:    # right
        if s[0] < (MAZE_W - 1) * UNIT:
            base_action[0] += UNIT
    elif action == 3:    # left
        if s[0] > UNIT:
            base_action[0] -= UNIT

    self.canvas.move(self.rect, base_action[0], base_action[1])  # move
    agent

    s_ = self.canvas.coords(self.rect)  # next state

    # reward function
    if s_ == self.canvas.coords(self.oval):
        reward = 1
        done = True
    elif s_ in [self.canvas.coords(self.hell1), self.canvas.coords
(self.hell2)]:
```

```
            reward = -1
            done = True
        else:
            reward = 0
            done = False

        return s_, reward, done

    def render(self):
        time.sleep(0.1)
        self.update()
```

The Entire Reinforcement Logic in Python

When you are implementing the algorithm in Python, the structure looks like the following. The content is in the repo.

```
import numpy as np
import pandas as pd

class RL(object):
    def __init__(self, action_space, learning_rate=0.01, reward_decay=0.9,
    e_greedy=0.9):
        self.actions = action_space  # a list
        self.lr = learning_rate
        self.gamma = reward_decay
        self.epsilon = e_greedy

        self.q_table = pd.DataFrame(columns=self.actions)

    def check_state_exist(self, state):
        if state not in self.q_table.index:
            # append new state to q table
            self.q_table = self.q_table.append(
                pd.Series(
                    [0]*len(self.actions),
                    index=self.q_table.columns,
                    name=state,
                )
            )

    def choose_action(self, observation):
        self.check_state_exist(observation)
        # action selection
        if np.random.rand() < self.epsilon:
            # choose best action
```

```
            state_action = self.q_table.ix[observation, :]
            state_action = state_action.reindex(np.random.permutation(state_
            action.index))     # some actions have the same value
            action = state_action.argmax()
        else:
            # choose random action
            action = np.random.choice(self.actions)
        return action

    def learn(self, *args):
        Pass


# off-policy
class QLearningTable(RL):
    def __init__(self, actions, learning_rate=0.01, reward_decay=0.9, e_
greedy=0.9):
        super(QLearningTable, self).__init__(actions, learning_rate, reward_
        decay, e_greedy)

    def learn(self, s, a, r, s_):
        self.check_state_exist(s_)
        q_predict = self.q_table.ix[s, a]
        if s_ != 'terminal':
            q_target = r + self.gamma * self.q_table.ix[s_, :].max()  # next
            state is not terminal
        else:
            q_target = r  # next state is terminal
        self.q_table.ix[s, a] += self.lr * (q_target - q_predict)  # update


# on-policy
class SarsaTable(RL):

    def __init__(self, actions, learning_rate=0.01, reward_decay=0.9, e_
greedy=0.9):
        super(SarsaTable, self).__init__(actions, learning_rate, reward_
        decay, e_greedy)

    def learn(self, s, a, r, s_, a_):
        self.check_state_exist(s_)
        q_predict = self.q_table.ix[s, a]
        if s_ != 'terminal':
            q_target = r + self.gamma * self.q_table.ix[s_, a_]  # next
            state is not terminal
        else:
            q_target = r  # next state is terminal
        self.q_table.ix[s, a] += self.lr * (q_target - q_predict)  # update
```

The learning process in its entirety looks like this in the code (RL_brain.py):

```python
from maze_env import Maze
from RL_brain import SarsaTable

def update():
    for episode in range(100):
        # initial observation
        observation = env.reset()

        # RL choose action based on observation
        action = RL.choose_action(str(observation))

        while True:
            # fresh env
            env.render()

            # RL take action and get next observation and reward
            observation_, reward, done = env.step(action)

            # RL choose action based on next observation
            action_ = RL.choose_action(str(observation_))

            # RL learn from this transition (s, a, r, s, a) ==> Sarsa
            RL.learn(str(observation), action, reward, str(observation_),
            action_)

            # swap observation and action
            observation = observation_
            action = action_

            # break while loop when end of this episode
            if done:
                break

    # end of game
    print('game over')
    env.destroy()

if __name__ == "__main__":
    env = Maze()
    RL = SarsaTable(actions=list(range(env.n_actions)))

    env.after(100, update)
    env.mainloop()
```

Let's run the program and check it.

You can do this in the Anaconda environment, as shown in Figure 2-57.

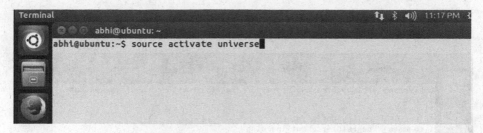

Figure 2-57. *Activating the environment*

You then have to consider the SARSA maze, as shown in Figure 2-58.

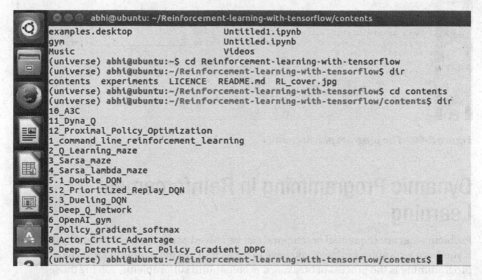

Figure 2-58. *Considering the SARSA maze*

Now you have to call the run_this.py file to get the program running, as shown in Figure 2-59.

```
(universe) abhi@ubuntu:~/Reinforcement-learning-with-tensorflow/contents$ cd 3_S
arsa_maze
(universe) abhi@ubuntu:~/Reinforcement-learning-with-tensorflow/contents/3_Sarsa
_maze$ dir
maze_env.py  __pycache__  RL_brain.py  run_this.py
(universe) abhi@ubuntu:~/Reinforcement-learning-with-tensorflow/contents/3_Sarsa
_maze$
```

Figure 2-59. *Running run_this.py*

To run the program from the terminal, use this command:

```
python run_this.py
```

After running the code, the program will play the maze, as shown in Figure 2-60.

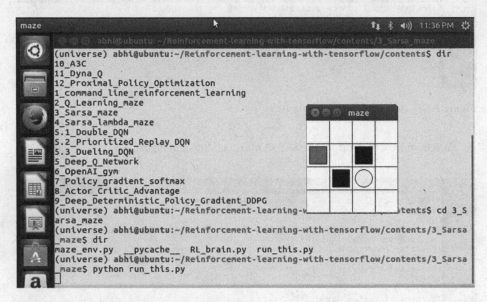

Figure 2-60. *The program playing maze*

Dynamic Programming in Reinforcement Learning

Problems that are sequential or temporal can be solved using dynamic programming. If you have a complex problem, you have to break it down into subproblems. Dynamic programming is the process of breaking a problem into subproblems, solving those subproblems, and finally combining them to solve the overall problem. The optimal substructure and the principle of optimality apply. The solution can be cached and reused. See Figure 2-61.

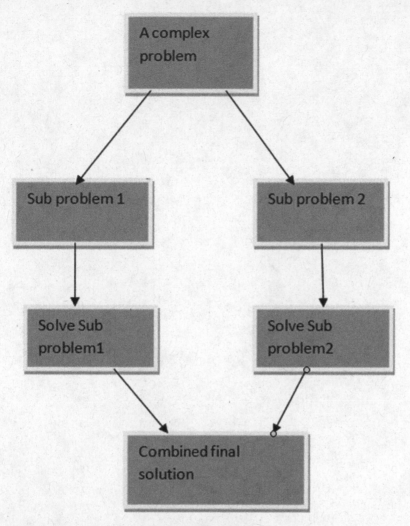

Figure 2-61. *Dynamic problem-solving approach*

Conclusion

This chapter went through different algorithms related to Reinforcement Learning. You also saw a simple example of Reinforcement Learning using Python. You then learned about SARSA with the help of an example in Python. The chapter ended by discussing dynamic programming basics.

CHAPTER 3

■■■

OpenAI Basics

This chapter introduces the world of OpenAI and uses it in relation to Reinforcement Learning.

First, we go through environments that are important to Reinforcement Learning. We talk about two supportive platforms that are useful for Reinforcement Learning—Google DeepMind and OpenAI, the latter of which is supported by Elon Musk. The completely open sourced OpenAI is discussed in this chapter and Google DeepMind is discussed in Chapter 6.

The chapter first covers OpenAI basics and then moves toward describing them and discusses the OpenAI Gym and OpenAI Universe environments. Then we cover installing OpenAI Gym and OpenAI Universe on the Ubuntu and Anaconda distributions. Finally, we discuss using OpenAI Gym and OpenAI Universe for the purpose of Reinforcement Learning.

Getting to Know OpenAI

To start, you need to access the OpenAI web site at https://openai.com/.

The web site is shown in Figure 3-1.

Figure 3-1. *The OpenAI web site*

A. Nandy and M. Biswas, *Reinforcement Learning*,
https://doi.org/10.1007/978-1-4842-3285-9_3

The OpenAI web site is full of content and resources. It has lots of resources for you to learn and research accordingly. Let's see schematically how OpenAI Gym and OpenAI Universe are connected. See Figure 3-2.

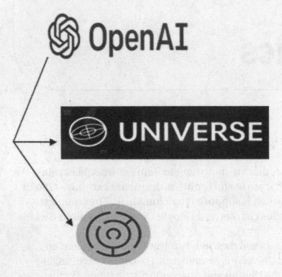

Figure 3-2. *OpenAI Gym and OpenAI Universe*

Figure 3-2 shows how OpenAI Gym and OpenAI Universe are connected, by using their icons.

The OpenAI Gym page of the web site is shown in Figure 3-3.

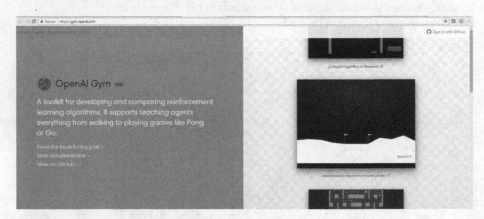

Figure 3-3. *OpenAI Gym web site*

OpenAI Gym is a toolkit that helps you run simulation games and scenarios to apply Reinforcement Learning as well as to apply Reinforcement Learning algorithms. It supports teaching agents for doing lots of activities, such as playing, walking, etc.

The OpenAI Universe web site is shown in Figure 3-4.

Figure 3-4. *The OpenAI Universe web site*

OpenAI Universe is a software platform that measures and trains an AI's general intelligence across different kinds of games and applications.

Installing OpenAI Gym and OpenAI Universe

In this section, you learn how to install OpenAI Gym and OpenAI Universe in an Ubuntu machine using version 16.04.

Go into the Anaconda environment to install OpenAI Gym from GitHub. See Figure 3-5.

```
(universe) openai@ubuntu:~$ cd ~
(universe) openai@ubuntu:~$ git clone https://github.com/openai/gym.git
Cloning into 'gym'...
remote: Counting objects: 5901, done.
remote: Total 5901 (delta 0), reused 0 (delta 0), pack-reused 5901
Receiving objects: 100% (5901/5901), 1.46 MiB | 437.00 KiB/s, done.
Resolving deltas: 100% (3977/3977), done.
Checking connectivity... done.
(universe) openai@ubuntu:~$ 
```

Figure 3-5. *Cloning OpenAI Gym*

You can clone and install OpenAI Gym from GitHub using this command:

```
$ source activate universe
(universe) $ cd ~
(universe) $ git clone https://github.com/openai/gym.git
(universe) $ cd gym
(universe) $ pip install -e '.[all]'
```

Now install OpenAI Universe as follows:

```
(universe) $ cd ~
(universe) $ git clone https://github.com/openai/universe.git
(universe) $ cd universe
(universe) $ pip install -e
```

The packages are being installed. Figure 3-6 shows the cloning process for OpenAI Universe.

```
(universe) openai@ubuntu:~$ cd gym
(universe) openai@ubuntu:~/gym$ pip install -e '.[all]'
Obtaining file:///home/openai/gym
Requirement already satisfied: numpy>=1.10.4 in /home/openai/anaconda3/envs/universe/lib/python3.5/site-packages (from gym==0.9.2)
Requirement already satisfied: requests>=2.0 in /home/openai/anaconda3/envs/universe/lib/python3.5/site-packages (from gym==0.9.2)
Requirement already satisfied: six in /home/openai/anaconda3/envs/universe/lib/python3.5/site-packages (from gym==0.9.2)
Collecting pyglet>=1.2.0 (from gym==0.9.2)
  Downloading pyglet-1.2.4-py3-none-any.whl (964kB)
    100% |████████████████████████████████| 972kB 270kB/s
Collecting pachi-py>=0.0.19 (from gym==0.9.2)
  Downloading pachi-py-0.0.21.tar.gz (1.1MB)
    100% |████████████████████████████████| 1.1MB 751kB/s
Collecting keras (from gym==0.9.2)
  Downloading Keras-2.0.8-py2.py3-none-any.whl (276kB)
    100% |████████████████████████████████| 276kB 1.2MB/s
Collecting theano (from gym==0.9.2)
  Downloading Theano-0.9.0.tar.gz (3.1MB)
    100% |████████████████████████████████| 3.1MB 271kB/s
Collecting mujoco_py<1.0.0,>=0.4.3 (from gym==0.9.2)
```

Figure 3-6. *Cloning OpenAI Universe*

The entire process, with all the important files, is downloaded, as shown in Figure 3-7.

```
Requirement already satisfied: Pillow in /home/openai/anaconda3/envs/universe/lib/python3.5/site-packages (from gym==0.9.2)
Requirement already satisfied: pyyaml in /home/openai/anaconda3/envs/universe/lib/python3.5/site-packages (from gym==0.9.2)
Requirement already satisfied: scipy>=0.14 in /home/openai/anaconda3/envs/universe/lib/python3.5/site-packages (from keras->gym==0.9.2)
Building wheels for collected packages: pachi-py, theano, mujoco-py, imageio, Box2D-kengz, PyOpenGL, atari-py
  Running setup.py bdist_wheel for pachi-py ... done
  Stored in directory: /home/openai/.cache/pip/wheels/48/46/12/3331c18c26bd673c6ae9facca5c6b262d18a8566ca1fe81b9f
  Running setup.py bdist_wheel for theano ... done
  Stored in directory: /home/openai/.cache/pip/wheels/d5/5b/93/433299b86e3e9b25f8f600e4e4ebf18e3beb7534ea518eba13
  Running setup.py bdist_wheel for mujoco-py ... done
  Stored in directory: /home/openai/.cache/pip/wheels/88/47/5a/b9809fb3596051e6317e78dbb03db1f0881f14501ef0c22018
  Running setup.py bdist_wheel for imageio ... done
  Stored in directory: /home/openai/.cache/pip/wheels/2a/87/cf/7c098611c6b49ceb0967ff9c22277a0d3ba6d9d6742068a33d
  Running setup.py bdist_wheel for Box2D-kengz ... done
  Stored in directory: /home/openai/.cache/pip/wheels/50/e8/e4/cec46723922533cc08ca9ec06da1a27b692832c61bbc430623
  Running setup.py bdist_wheel for PyOpenGL ... done
  Stored in directory: /home/openai/.cache/pip/wheels/1c/17/50/f69d63e0a8169fb890f5a167817a73391be85d30e86fd29504
  Running setup.py bdist_wheel for atari-py ... done
  Stored in directory: /home/openai/.cache/pip/wheels/9d/9a/35/e8c7372d2677e509571935b94142c1876ab6319e0cd12789e5
Successfully built pachi-py theano mujoco-py imageio Box2D-kengz PyOpenGL atari-py
Installing collected packages: pyglet, pachi-py, keras, theano, PyOpenGL, mujoco-py, imageio, Box2D-kengz, atari-py, gym
  Running setup.py develop for gym
Successfully installed Box2D-kengz-2.3.3 PyOpenGL-3.1.0 atari-py-0.1.1 gym imageio-2.2.0 keras-2.0.8 mujoco-py-0.5.7 pachi-py-0.0.21 pyglet-1.2.4 theano-0.9.0
(universe) openai@ubuntu:~/gym$
```

Figure 3-7. *Important steps of the installation process*

The process installation continues, as shown in Figure 3-8.

```
    100% |████████████████████████████████| 81kB 6.1MB/s
Requirement already satisfied: setuptools in /home/openai/anaconda3/envs/universe/lib/python3.5/site-packages (from zope.interface>=4.0.1->twisted>=16.5.0->universe==0.21.5)
Collecting attrs (from Automat>=0.3.0->twisted>=16.5.0->universe==0.21.5)
  Downloading attrs-17.2.0-py2.py3-none-any.whl
Building wheels for collected packages: fastzbarlight, go-vncdriver, twisted, ujson
  Running setup.py bdist_wheel for fastzbarlight ... done
  Stored in directory: /home/openai/.cache/pip/wheels/21/44/64/5be2c657e496c2322d6cbaf8a1b0f8d61513550870786fd297f
  Running setup.py bdist_wheel for go-vncdriver ... done
  Stored in directory: /home/openai/.cache/pip/wheels/13/24/dc/91144d44ef4bc1c2b2f01138c79a9361edbf574d33d2c7192d
  Running setup.py bdist_wheel for twisted ... done
  Stored in directory: /home/openai/.cache/pip/wheels/57/08/00/28a9a06f8ee9f54260fb5949aed2ea9b0442e8a87b757aa7ce
  Running setup.py bdist_wheel for ujson ... done
  Stored in directory: /home/openai/.cache/pip/wheels/9e/9b/d0/df92053bbb2064c15d8ee5b99e3f2eb00ad34444db0922b2f
Successfully built fastzbarlight go-vncdriver twisted ujson
Installing collected packages: txaio, autobahn, docker-pycreds, websocket-client, requests, docker-py, fastzbarlight, go-vncdriver, zope.interface, constantly, incremental, attrs, Automat, hyperlink
  ted, ujson, universe
  Found existing installation: requests 2.14.2
    Uninstalling requests-2.14.2:
      Successfully uninstalled requests-2.14.2
  Running setup.py develop for universe
Successfully installed Automat-0.6.0 attrs-17.2.0 autobahn-17.8.1 constantly-15.1.0 docker-py-1.10.3 docker-pycreds-0.2.1 fastzbarlight-0.0.14 go-vncdriver-0.4.19 hyperlink-17.3.1 incremental-17.5.0
sts-2.10.0 twisted-17.5.0 txaio-2.9.1 ujson-1.35 universe websocket-client-0.44.0 zope.interface-4.4.2
(universe) openai@ubuntu:~/gym$
```

Figure 3-8. *More steps of the installation process*

In the next section, you learn how to start working in the OpenAI Gym and OpenAI environment.

Working with OpenAI Gym and OpenAI

The OpenAI cycle for a sample process is shown in Figure 3-9.

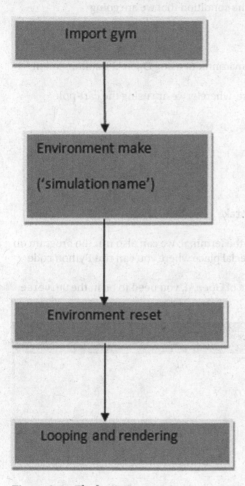

Figure 3-9. *The basic OpenAI Gym structure*

The process works this way. We are dealing with a simple Gym project. The language of choice here is Python, but we are more focused on the logic of how an environment is being utilized.

1. We import the Gym library.

2. We create an instance of the simulation to perform using the make function.

3. We reset the simulation so that the condition that we are going to apply can be realized.

4. We do looping and then render.

The output is a simulated result of the environment using OpenAI Reinforcement Learning techniques.

The program using Python is shown here, whereby we are using the cart-pole simulation example:

```python
import gym
 env = gym.make('CartPole-v0')
env.reset()
for _ in range(1000):
env.render()
env.step(env.action_space.sample()) # take a random action
```

The program that we created runs from the terminal; we can also run the program on a jupyter notebook. Jupyter notebook is a special place where you can run Python code very easily.

To use the properties or the file structure of OpenAI, you need to be in the universe directory, as shown in Figure 3-10.

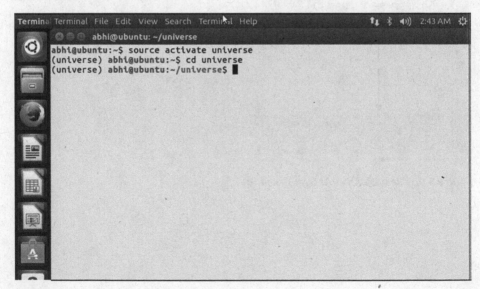

Figure 3-10. *Inside the universe directory*

To work with the Gym components, you need to get inside the gym directory, as shown in Figure 3-11.

Figure 3-11. *Inside the gym directory*

You then need to open the jupyter notebook. Enter this command from the terminal to open the jupyter notebook (see Figure 3-12):

```
jupyter notebook
```

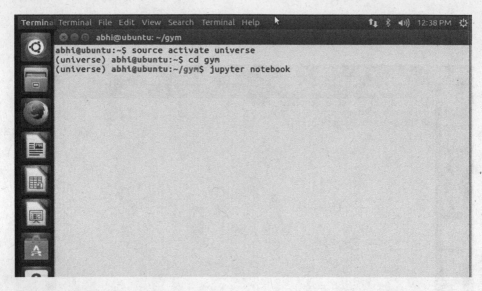

Figure 3-12. *Using the jupyter notebook*

When you issue the command, the jupyter notebook engine side-loads essential components so that everything related to the jupyter notebook is loaded, as shown in Figure 3-13.

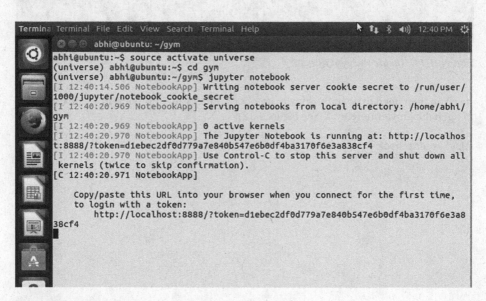

Figure 3-13. *The essential components of jupyter notebooks*

Once the jupyter notebook is loaded, you will see that the interface has an option for working with Python files. The type of distribution you have for Python is shown in the interface. Figure 3-14 shows that Python 3 is installed in this case.

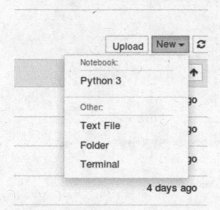

Figure 3-14. *Opening a new Python file*

You can now start working with the Gym interface and start importing Gym libraries, as shown in Figure 3-15.

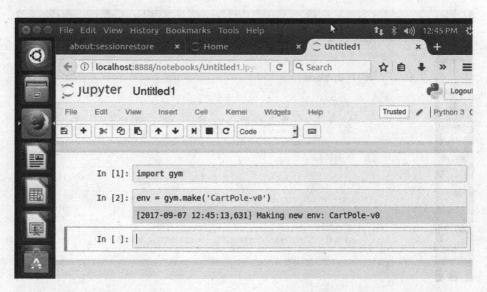

Figure 3-15. *Working with Gym inside the jupyter notebook*

The process continues until the program flow is completed. Figure 3-16 shows the process flow.

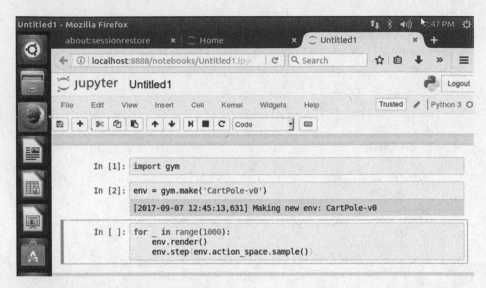

Figure 3-16. *The flow of the program*

After being reset, the environment shows an array, as shown in Figure 3-17.

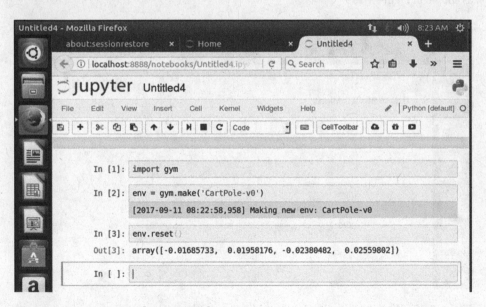

Figure 3-17. *An array is being created*

Figure 3-18 shows the simulation. The cart-pole shifts by a margin that's reflected by the array's values.

Figure 3-18. *The simulation in action*

More Simulations

This section shows you how to try different simulations. There are many different environment types in OpenAI. One of them is the logarithmic type, discussed next.

There is variety of tasks involved in algorithms. Run this code to include the environment in the jupyter notebook (see Figure 3-19):

```
import gym
env = gym.make('Copy-v0')
env.reset()
env.render()
```

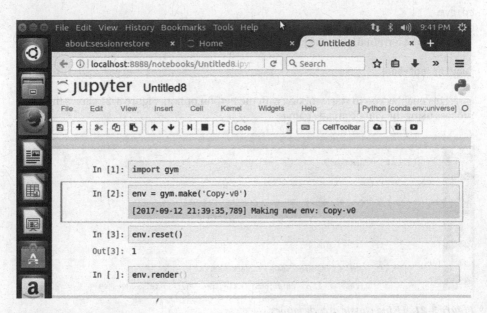

Figure 3-19. *Including the environment in the jupyter notebook*

The output looks like Figure 3-20. The prime motive for this simulation is to copy symbols from an input sequence.

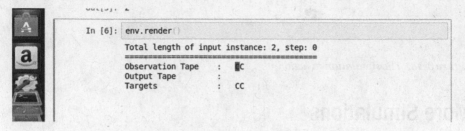

Figure 3-20. *The output after running the render function*

This section uses an example of classic arcade games. First, open the required Anaconda environment using the following command:

```
source activate universe
```

Then go to the appropriate directory, say gym:

```
cd gym
```

From the terminal, start the jupyter notebook using this command:

```
jupyter notebook
```

This enables you to start working with the Python option. Figure 3-21 shows the process using the classic arcade games.

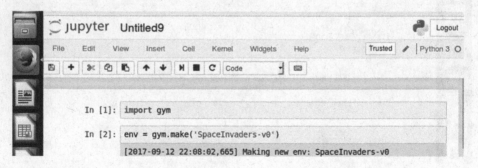

Figure 3-21. *Using classic arcade games*

After using env.reset(), an array is generated, as shown in Figure 3-22.

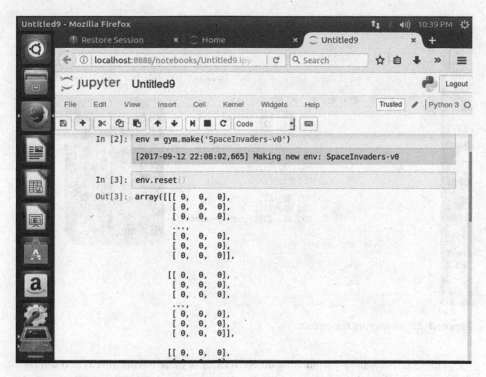

Figure 3-22. *The array is being created*

If you use `env.render()`, you'll generate the output shown in Figure 3-23.

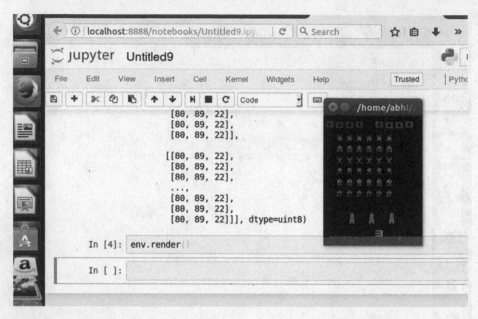

Figure 3-23. *Rendering the output*

This example is simply simulating different kinds of game environments and setting them up for Reinforcement Learning.

Here is the code to simulate the Space Invaders game:

```
import gym
env = gym.make('SpaceInvaders-v0')
env.reset()
env.render()
```

In the next section, you will learn how to work with OpenAI Universe.

OpenAI Universe

In this example, you will be using the jupyter notebook to simulate a game environment and then will apply Reinforcement Learning to it. Go to the `universe` directory and start the jupyter notebook.

```
import gym
import universe  # register the universe environments

env = gym.make('flashgames.DuskDrive-v0')
```

```
env.configure(remotes=1)  # automatically creates a local docker container
observation_n = env.reset()

while True:
  action_n = [[('KeyEvent', 'ArrowUp', True)] for ob in observation_n]  #
  your agent here
  observation_n, reward_n, done_n, info = env.step(action_n)
  env.render()
```

Figure 3-24 shows the code needed to set up the environment for the DuskDrive game.

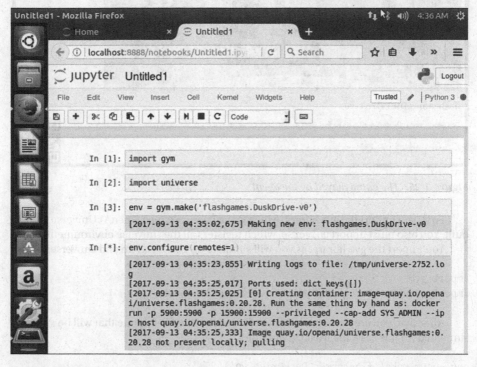

Figure 3-24. Setting up the environment for the DuskDrive game

Now it will access the image and start the image remotely. It will run the game and start playing remotely with the help of an agent. See Figure 3-25.

Figure 3-25. *The game played by the agent*

First, you import the gym library, which is the base on which OpenAI Universe is built. You also must import `universe`, which registers all the Universe environments.

You import the gym library, as you will simulate on OpenAI Gym and Universe:

```
import gym
import universe # register the universe environments
```

After that, you create an environment for loading the Flash game that will be simulated (in this case, the DuskDrive game).

```
env = gym.make('flashgames.DuskDrive-v0')
env = gym.make('flashgames.DuskDrive-v0')
```

You call `configure`, which creates a dockerized environment for running the simulation locally.

```
env.configure(remotes=1)
```

You then call `Env.reset ()` to instantiate the proper simulation environment asynchronously

```
observation_n = env.reset()
```

You then define the `keyEvent` and `Arrowup` actions to move the car in the simulated environment:

```
action_n = [[('KeyEvent', 'ArrowUp', True)] for ob in observation_n]
```

To get rewards and to check the status of the episodes, you use the following code and render accordingly.

```
observation_n, reward_n, done_n, info = env.step(action_n)
env.render()
```

Conclusion

This chapter explained the details of OpenAI. First, it described OpenAI in general and then described OpenAI Gym and OpenAI Universe.

We touched on installing OpenAI Gym and OpenAI Universe and then started coding for them using the Python language. Finally, we looked at some examples of both OpenAI Gym and OpenAI Universe.

CHAPTER 4

■ ■ ■

Applying Python to Reinforcement Learning

This chapter explores the world of Reinforcement Learning in terms of Python. First we go through Q learning with Python and then cover a more in-depth analysis of Reinforcement Learning. We start off by going through Q learning in terms of Python. Then we describe Swarm intelligence in Python, with an introduction to what exactly Swarm intelligence is. The chapter also covers the Markov decision process (MDP) toolbox.

Finally, you will be implementing a Game AI and will apply Reinforcement Learning to it. The chapter will be a good experience, so let's begin!

Q Learning with Python

Let's start with a maze problem. The object of the game is to reach the yellow circle while avoiding the black squares. Figure 4-1 shows the maze. We use the numpy library in this example.

© Abhishek Nandy and Manisha Biswas 2018
A. Nandy and M. Biswas, *Reinforcement Learning*,
https://doi.org/10.1007/978-1-4842-3285-9_4

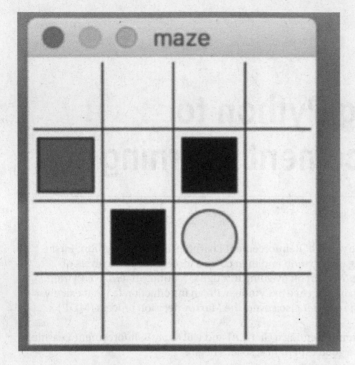

Figure 4-1. *The maze that demonstrates Q learning*

We have to choose an action based on the Q table, which is why we have the function called `choose_action`. When we want to move from one state to another, we apply the decision-making process to the `choose_action` method as follows.

```
def choose_action(self,observation):
```

The learning process function takes the transition from state, award, reward and goes to the next state.

```
def check_State_exist(self,state)
```

The `check_State_exist` function allows us to check if the state exists and then to append it to the Q table if it does.

The content of the function we have discussed is actually for `RL_brain`, which is the basis of the project. The rules are updated for Q learning, as shown in the `run _this.py` file.

The Maze Environment Python File

The maze environment Python file, shown here, lists all the concepts for making moves. We declare rewards as well as ability to take the next step.

```
"""
Reinforcement learning maze example.

Red rectangle:          explorer.
Black rectangles:       hells          [reward = -1].
Yellow bin circle:      paradise       [reward = +1].
All other states:       ground         [reward = 0].

This script is the environment part of this example. The RL is in RL_brain.
py.

View more on my tutorial page: https://morvanzhou.github.io/tutorials/
"""

import numpy as np
import time
import sys
if sys.version_info.major == 2:
    import Tkinter as tk
else:
    import tkinter as tk

UNIT = 40   # pixels
MAZE_H = 4  # grid height
MAZE_W = 4  # grid width

class Maze(tk.Tk, object):
    def __init__(self):
        super(Maze, self).__init__()
        self.action_space = ['u', 'd', 'l', 'r']
        self.n_actions = len(self.action_space)
        self.title('maze')
        self.geometry('{0}x{1}'.format(MAZE_H * UNIT, MAZE_H * UNIT))
        self._build_maze()

    def _build_maze(self):
        self.canvas = tk.Canvas(self, bg='white',
                        height=MAZE_H * UNIT,
                        width=MAZE_W * UNIT)
```

```python
        # create grids
        for c in range(0, MAZE_W * UNIT, UNIT):
            x0, y0, x1, y1 = c, 0, c, MAZE_H * UNIT
            self.canvas.create_line(x0, y0, x1, y1)
        for r in range(0, MAZE_H * UNIT, UNIT):
            x0, y0, x1, y1 = 0, r, MAZE_H * UNIT, r
            self.canvas.create_line(x0, y0, x1, y1)

        # create origin
        origin = np.array([20, 20])

        # hell
        hell1_center = origin + np.array([UNIT * 2, UNIT])
        self.hell1 = self.canvas.create_rectangle(
            hell1_center[0] - 15, hell1_center[1] - 15,
            hell1_center[0] + 15, hell1_center[1] + 15,
            fill='black')
        # hell
        hell2_center = origin + np.array([UNIT, UNIT * 2])
        self.hell2 = self.canvas.create_rectangle(
            hell2_center[0] - 15, hell2_center[1] - 15,
            hell2_center[0] + 15, hell2_center[1] + 15,
            fill='black')

        # create oval
        oval_center = origin + UNIT * 2
        self.oval = self.canvas.create_oval(
            oval_center[0] - 15, oval_center[1] - 15,
            oval_center[0] + 15, oval_center[1] + 15,
            fill='yellow')

        # create red rect
        self.rect = self.canvas.create_rectangle(
            origin[0] - 15, origin[1] - 15,
            origin[0] + 15, origin[1] + 15,
            fill='red')

        # pack all
        self.canvas.pack()

    def reset(self):
        self.update()
        time.sleep(0.5)
        self.canvas.delete(self.rect)
        origin = np.array([20, 20])
        self.rect = self.canvas.create_rectangle(
            origin[0] - 15, origin[1] - 15,
            origin[0] + 15, origin[1] + 15,
```

```
                fill='red')
        # return observation
        return self.canvas.coords(self.rect)

    def step(self, action):
        s = self.canvas.coords(self.rect)
        base_action = np.array([0, 0])
        if action == 0:    # up
            if s[1] > UNIT:
                base_action[1] -= UNIT
        elif action == 1:    # down
            if s[1] < (MAZE_H - 1) * UNIT:
                base_action[1] += UNIT
        elif action == 2:    # right
            if s[0] < (MAZE_W - 1) * UNIT:
                base_action[0] += UNIT

        elif action == 3:    # left
            if s[0] > UNIT:
                base_action[0] -= UNIT

        self.canvas.move(self.rect, base_action[0], base_action[1])  # move
        agent

        s_ = self.canvas.coords(self.rect)  # next state

        # reward function
        if s_ == self.canvas.coords(self.oval):
            reward = 1
            done = True
        elif s_ in [self.canvas.coords(self.hell1), self.canvas.coords(self.
        hell2)]:
            reward = -1
            done = True
        else:
            reward = 0
            done = False

        return s_, reward, done

    def render(self):
        time.sleep(0.1)
        self.update()

def update():
    for t in range(10):
        s = env.reset()
        while True:
```

```
            env.render()
            a = 1
            s, r, done = env.step(a)
            if done:
                break

if __name__ == '__main__':
    env = Maze()
    env.after(100, update)
    env.mainloop()
```

The RL_Brain Python File

Now for the RL_brain Python file. We define the Q learning table structure that is generated while moving from one state to another. In the QLearningTable class, we structure the way the entire maze learns. We also declare hyperparameters for learning and determine the rate at which the program learns in the next chunk of code:

```
import numpy as np

import pandas as pd

class QLearningTable:
    def __init__(self, actions, learning_rate=0.01, reward_decay=0.9, e_
    greedy=0.9):
        self.actions = actions  # a list
        self.lr = learning_rate
        self.gamma = reward_decay
        self.epsilon = e_greedy
        self.q_table = pd.DataFrame(columns=self.actions)

    def choose_action(self, observation):
        self.check_state_exist(observation)
        # action selection
        if np.random.uniform() < self.epsilon:
            # choose best action
            state_action = self.q_table.ix[observation, :]
            state_action = state_action.reindex(np.random.permutation(state_
            action.index))     # some actions have same value
            action = state_action.argmax()
        else:
            # choose random action
            action = np.random.choice(self.actions)
        return action

    def learn(self, s, a, r, s_):
        self.check_state_exist(s_)
```

```
        q_predict = self.q_table.ix[s, a]
        if s_ != 'terminal':
            q_target = r + self.gamma * self.q_table.ix[s_, :].max()  # next
            state is not terminal
        else:
            q_target = r  # next state is terminal
        self.q_table.ix[s, a] += self.lr * (q_target - q_predict)  # update

    def check_state_exist(self, state):
        if state not in self.q_table.index:
            # append new state to q table
            self.q_table = self.q_table.append(
                pd.Series(
                    [0]*len(self.actions),
                    index=self.q_table.columns,
                    name=state,
                )
            )
```

Updating the Function

This code segment declares a function that receives updates on the movement in the maze from one state to another. It also gives out rewards when the player transitions from one state to another.

```
from maze_env import Maze

from RL_brain import QLearningTable

def update():
    for episode in range(100):
        # initial observation
        observation = env.reset()

        while True:
            # fresh env
            env.render()

            # RL choose action based on observation
            action = RL.choose_action(str(observation))

            # RL take action and get next observation and reward
            observation_, reward, done = env.step(action)

            # RL learn from this transition
            RL.learn(str(observation), action, reward, str(observation_))
```

```
            # swap observation
            observation = observation_

            # break while loop when end of this episode
            if done:
                break

    # end of game
    print('game over')
    env.destroy()

if __name__ == "__main__":
    env = Maze()
    RL = QLearningTable(actions=list(range(env.n_actions)))

    env.after(100, update)
    env.mainloop()
```

If you get inside the folder, you'll see the run_this.py file and can get the output, as shown in Figure 4-2.

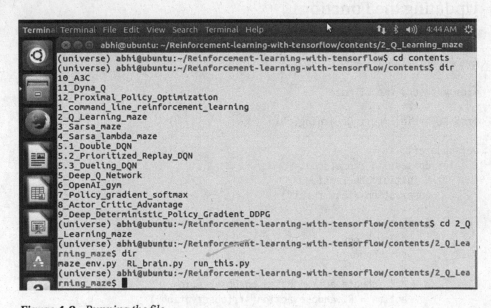

Figure 4-2. *Running the file*

Figure 4-3 shows the code running.

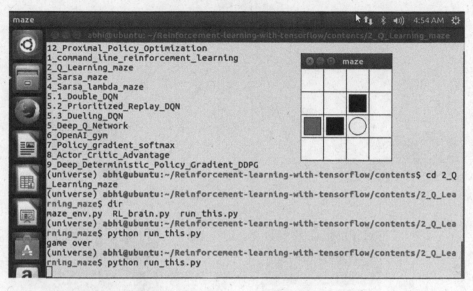

Figure 4-3. *The maze file being run*

Using the MDP Toolbox in Python

The MDP toolbox provides classes and functions for the resolution of discrete time Markov decision processes. The list of algorithms that have been implemented includes backwards induction, linear programming, policy iteration, Q learning, and value iteration along with several variations.

The following are the features of the MDP toolbox (see Figure 4-4):

- Eight MDP algorithms

- Fast array manipulation using NumPy

- Full sparse matrix support using Scipy's sparse package

- Optional linear programming support using cvxopt

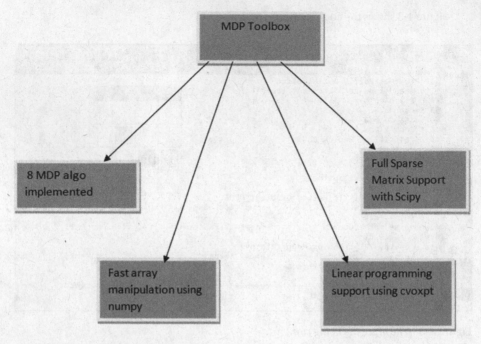

Figure 4-4. *MDP toolbox features*

Next, you see how to install and configure MDP toolbox for Python. First, switch to the Anaconda environment, as shown in Figure 4-5.

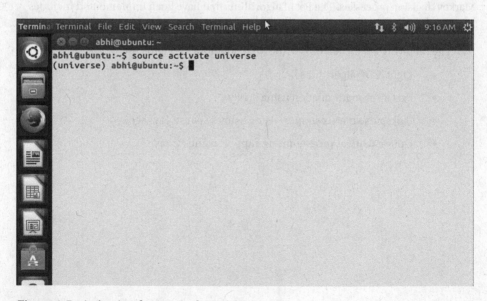

Figure 4-5. *Activating the Anaconda environment*

Now install the dependencies using this command (see Figure 4-6):

```
sudo apt-get install python3-numpy python3-scipy liblapack-dev libatlas-
base-dev libgsl0-dev fftw-dev libglpk-dev libdsdp-dev
```

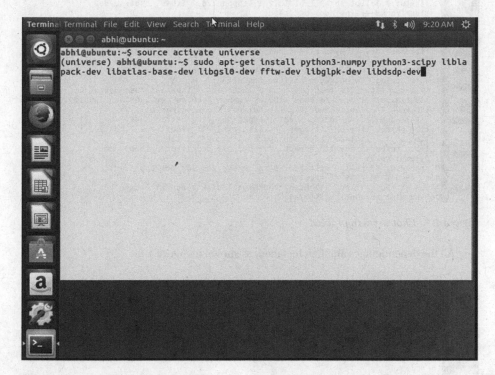

Figure 4-6. *Installing the dependencies*

When it asks you if it should install the dependencies, choose yes, as shown in Figure 4-7.

Figure 4-7. *Choose yes to proceed*

All the dependencies are then installed, as shown in Figure 4-8.

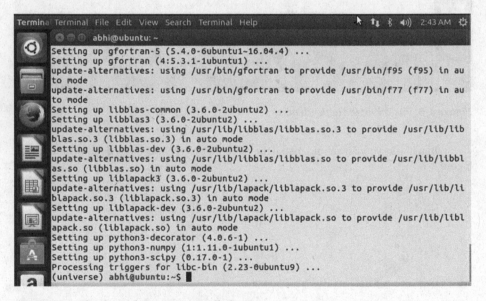

Figure 4-8. *The dependencies are installed*

Now you can go ahead and install the MDP toolbox, as shown in Figure 4-9.

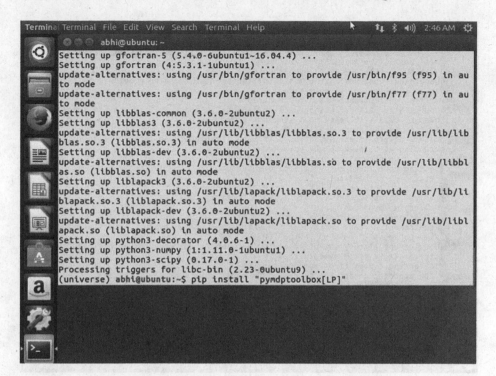

Figure 4-9. *Installing the MDP toolbox*

The important packages are being installed, as shown in Figure 4-10.

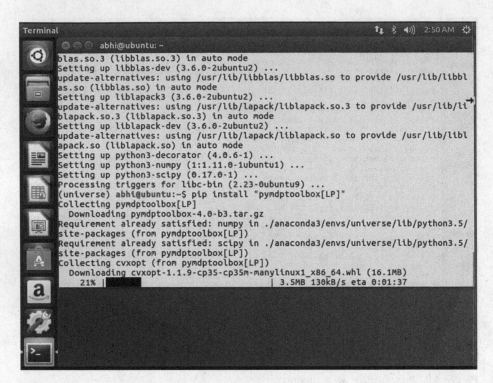

Figure 4-10. *Installing the important packages*

If everything works as expected, you'll get all the packages installed, as shown in Figure 4-11.

Figure 4-11. *All the packages have been installed*

Now you need to clone the repo from GitHub (see Figure 4-12):

```
git clone https://github.com/sawcordwell/pymdptoolbox.git
```

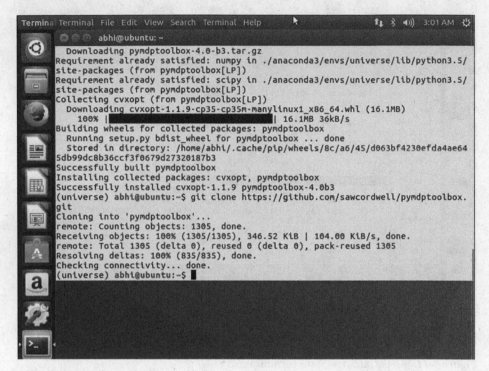

Figure 4-12. *Cloning the repo*

Switch to the mdptoolbox folder to see the details shown in Figure 4-13.

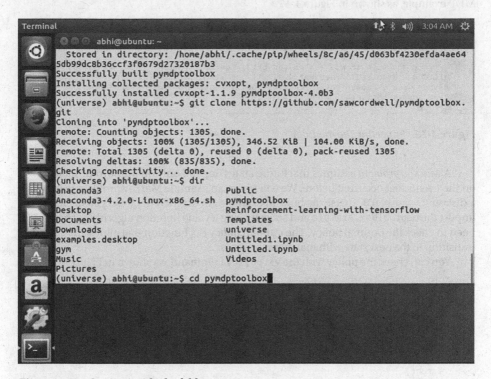

Figure 4-13. *Getting inside the folder*

You now need to switch to Python mode, as shown in Figure 4-14.

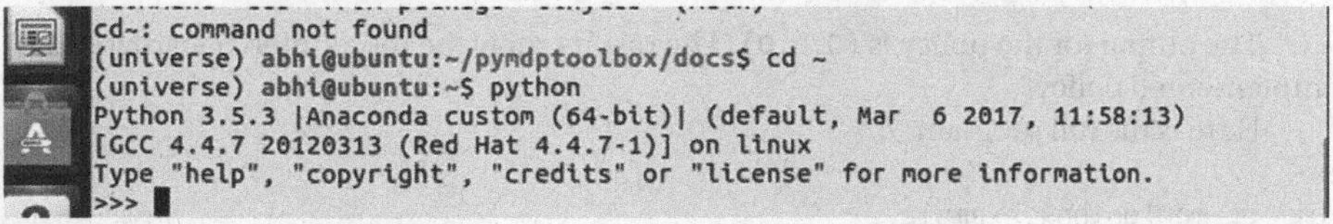

Figure 4-14. *Inside Python mode*

We will now use an example to see how the MDP toolbox works. First, import the MDP example, as shown in Figure 4-15.

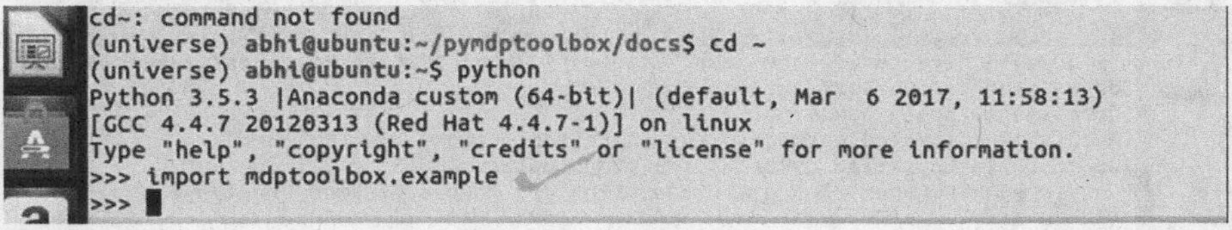

```
cd~: command not found
(universe) abhi@ubuntu:~/pymdptoolbox/docs$ cd ~
(universe) abhi@ubuntu:~$ python
Python 3.5.3 |Anaconda custom (64-bit)| (default, Mar  6 2017, 11:58:13)
[GCC 4.4.7 20120313 (Red Hat 4.4.7-1)] on linux
Type "help", "copyright", "credits" or "license" for more information.
>>> import mdptoolbox.example
>>>
```

Figure 4-15. *Importing the modules*

A *Markov problem* assumes that future states depend only on the current state, not on the events that occurred before. We will set up an example Markov problem using a discount value of 0.8. To use the built-in examples in the MDP toolbox, you need to import the mdptoolbox.example and solve it using a value iteration algorithm. Then you'll need to check the optimal policy. The *optimal policy* is a function that allows the state to transition to the next state with maximum rewards.

You can check the policy with the vi.policy command, as shown in Figure 4-16.

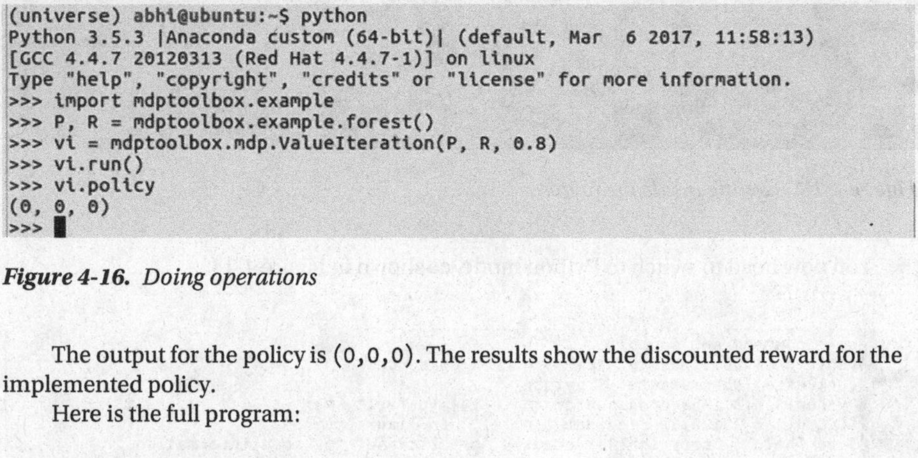

```
(universe) abhi@ubuntu:~$ python
Python 3.5.3 |Anaconda custom (64-bit)| (default, Mar  6 2017, 11:58:13)
[GCC 4.4.7 20120313 (Red Hat 4.4.7-1)] on linux
Type "help", "copyright", "credits" or "license" for more information.
>>> import mdptoolbox.example
>>> P, R = mdptoolbox.example.forest()
>>> vi = mdptoolbox.mdp.ValueIteration(P, R, 0.8)
>>> vi.run()
>>> vi.policy
(0, 0, 0)
>>>
```

Figure 4-16. *Doing operations*

The output for the policy is (0,0,0). The results show the discounted reward for the implemented policy.

Here is the full program:

```
import mdptoolbox.example
P, R = mdptoolbox.example.forest()
vi = mdptoolbox.mdp.ValueIteration(P, R, 0.8)
vi.run()
vi.policy # result is (0, 0, 0)
```

Let's consider another example. First you need to import the toolbox and the toolbox example. Using the import example, you are bringing in the built-in examples that are in the MDP toolbox (see Figure 4-17).

```
import mdptoolbox, mdptoolbox.example
```

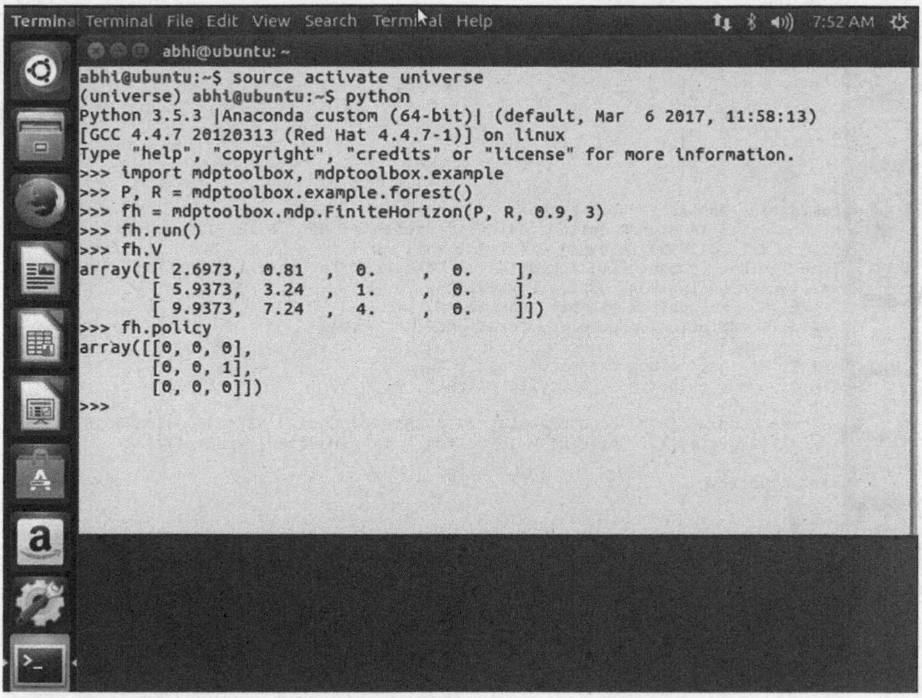

Figure 4-17. *Another example of MDP*

We implemented verbose mode in the previous example so we can display the current stage and policy transpose.

```
>>> import mdptoolbox, mdptoolbox.example
>>> P, R = mdptoolbox.example.forest()
>>> fh = mdptoolbox.mdp.FiniteHorizon(P, R, 0.9, 3)
>>> fh.run()
>>> fh.V
array([[ 2.6973, 0.81 , 0. , 0. ],
[ 5.9373, 3.24 , 1. , 0. ],
[ 9.9373, 7.24 , 4. , 0. ]])
>>> fh.policy
array([[0, 0, 0],
[0, 0, 1],
[0, 0, 0]])
```

The next example is also in verbose mode and each iteration displays the number of different actions between policy n-1 and n (see Figure 4-18).

```
Terminal Terminal File Edit View Search Terminal Help          t↓ ⋇ ◀)) 8:40 AM ⋭
  ⊗⊝⊕  abhi@ubuntu: ~
        [ 5.9373,  3.24 ,  1.   ,  0.    ],
        [ 9.9373,  7.24 ,  4.   ,  0.    ]])
>>> fh.policy
array([[0, 0, 0],
       [0, 0, 1],
       [0, 0, 0]])
>>>
(universe) abhi@ubuntu:~$ python
Python 3.5.3 |Anaconda custom (64-bit)| (default, Mar  6 2017, 11:58:13)
[GCC 4.4.7 20120313 (Red Hat 4.4.7-1)] on linux
Type "help", "copyright", "credits" or "license" for more information.
>>> import mdptoolbox, mdptoolbox.example
>>> P, R = mdptoolbox.example.rand(10, 3)
>>> pi = mdptoolbox.mdp.PolicyIteration(P, R, 0.9)
>>> pi.run()
>>> P, R = mdptoolbox.example.forest()
>>> pi = mdptoolbox.mdp.PolicyIteration(P, R, 0.9)
>>> pi.run()
>>> expected = (26.244000000000014, 29.484000000000016, 33.484000000000016)
>>> all(expected[k] - pi.V[k] < 1e-12 for k in range(len(expected)))
True
>>> pi.policy
(0, 0, 0)
>>>
```

Figure 4-18. *Policy between n-1 and n*

We are getting help from the built-in example of MDP, where we are trying to find the discounted MDP using a value iteration. As is the case with MDP, some of the values are randomly generated by using rand(10,3) and some of the values are provided by the decision-making process.

We try to solve an MDP by applying RL with a value iteration in this example:

```
>>> import mdptoolbox, mdptoolbox.example
>>> P, R = mdptoolbox.example.rand(10, 3)
>>> pi = mdptoolbox.mdp.PolicyIteration(P, R, 0.9)
>>> pi.run()
>>> P, R = mdptoolbox.example.forest()
>>> pi = mdptoolbox.mdp.PolicyIteration(P, R, 0.9)
>>> pi.run()
>>> expected = (26.244000000000014, 29.484000000000016, 33.484000000000016)
>>> all(expected[k] - pi.V[k] < 1e-12 for k in range(len(expected)))
    True
8.2. Markov Decision Process (MDP) Toolbox: mdp module 21
Python Markov Decision Process Toolbox Documentation, Release 4.0-b4
>>> pi.policy
(0, 0, 0)
```

108

Understanding Swarm Intelligence

Swarm intelligence is an important part of AI. It is the collective behavior of a decentralized, self-organized system, whether it be natural or artificial.

Swarm intelligence typically consists of a population of simple agents or *boids* (artificial life programs) interacting locally with one another and with their environment, as illustrated in Figure 4-19.

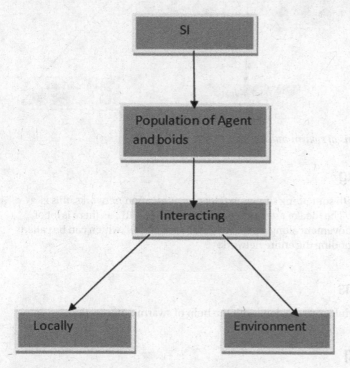

Figure 4-19. *Swarm intelligence interactions*

Applications of Swarm Intelligence

Figure 4-20 shows some applications of swarm intelligence.

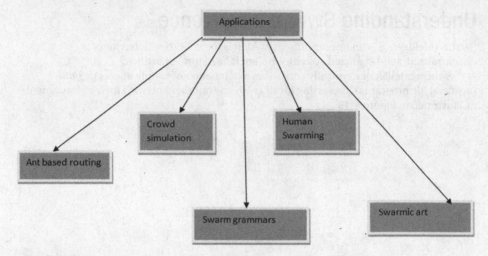

Figure 4-20. *Applications of swarm intelligence*

Ant-Based Routing

When you are dealing with something similar to telecommunication networks, this is called *ant-based routing*. The idea of ant based routing is based on RL, as there is lot of forward and backward movement along a particular network packet, which can be called the ant. This results in flooding the entire network.

Crowd Simulations

In the movies, crowd simulations are done with the help of swarm optimization.

Human Swarming

The concept of human swarming is based on the collective usage of different minds to predict an answer. It's when all of the brains of different human beings attempt to find a particular solution to a complex problem. Using collective brains in the form of human swarming results in more accurate results.

Swarm Grammars

Swarm grammars are particular characteristics that act as different swarms working together to get varied results. The results can be similar to art or architecture.

Swarmic Art

Combining different characteristics of swarm behaviors between different species of birds and fish can lead to swarmic art that shows patterns in swarm behavior.

Before we cover swarm intelligence in more detail, we touch on the Rastrigin function. Swarm optimization is based on different functions, one of which is the Rastrigin function, so you need to understand how it works.

The Rastrigin Function

In mathematical optimization problems, the Rastrigin function is a nonconvex function used as a performance test problem for optimization algorithms.

The formula is shown in Figure 4-21 and Figure 4-22 shows its typical output.

On an n-dimensional domain it is defined by:

$$f(\mathbf{x}) = An + \sum_{i=1}^{n} \left[x_i^2 - A \cos(2\pi x_i) \right]$$

where $A = 10$ and $x_i \in [-5.12, 5.12]$. It has a global minimum at $\mathbf{x} = 0$ where $f(\mathbf{x}) = 0$.

Figure 4-21. *Depiction of the Rastrigin function*

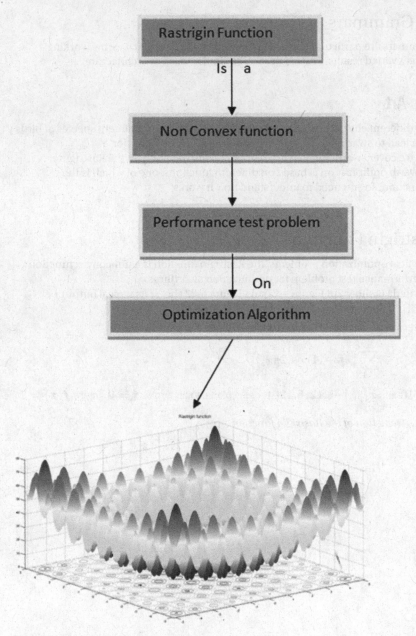

Figure 4-22. *Rastrigin function output*

Let's get started with using the Rastrigin function in Python.

You need to activate the Anaconda environment first:

```
abhi@ubuntu:~$ source activate universe
(universe) abhi@ubuntu:~$
```

Now switch to Python mode:

```
(universe) abhi@ubuntu:~$ python
Python 3.5.3 |Anaconda custom (64-bit)| (default, Mar  6 2017, 11:58:13)
[GCC 4.4.7 20120313 (Red Hat 4.4.7-1)] on linux
Type "help", "copyright", "credits" or "license" for more information.
>>>
```

As we start building important libraries, Python will cache them if they are not created, as shown in Figure 4-23.

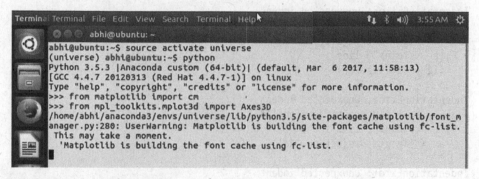

Figure 4-23. *Cache being created*

The entire flow of the Python program is as follows:

```
python
Python 3.5.3 |Anaconda custom (64-bit)| (default, Mar  6 2017, 11:58:13)
[GCC 4.4.7 20120313 (Red Hat 4.4.7-1)] on linux
Type "help", "copyright", "credits" or "license" for more information.
>>> from matplotlib import cm
>>> from mpl_toolkits.mplot3d import Axes3D
/home/abhi/anaconda3/envs/universe/lib/python3.5/site-packages/matplotlib/
font_manager.py:280: UserWarning: Matplotlib is building the font cache
using fc-list. This may take a moment.
  'Matplotlib is building the font cache using fc-list. '
>>> import math
>>> import matplotlib.pyplot as plt
>>> import numpy as np
>>> def rastrigin(*X, **kwargs):
...     A = kwargs.get('A', 10)
```

```
...        return A + sum([(x**2 - A * np.cos(2 * math.pi * x)) for x in X])
...
>>> if __name__ == '__main__':
...     X = np.linspace(-4, 4, 200)
...     Y = np.linspace(-4, 4, 200)
...
>>>     X, Y = np.meshgrid(X, Y)
  File "<stdin>", line 1
    X, Y = np.meshgrid(X, Y)
    ^
IndentationError: unexpected indent
>>>
>>>     Z = rastrigin(X, Y, A=10)
  File "<stdin>", line 1
    Z = rastrigin(X, Y, A=10)
    ^
IndentationError: unexpected indent
>>>
>>>     fig = plt.figure()
  File "<stdin>", line 1
    fig = plt.figure()
    ^
IndentationError: unexpected indent
>>>     ax = fig.gca(projection='3d')
  File "<stdin>", line 1
    ax = fig.gca(projection='3d')
    ^
IndentationError: unexpected indent
>>>
>>>     ax.plot_surface(X, Y, Z, rstride=1, cstride=1, cmap=cm.plasma,
linewidth=0, antialiased=False)
  File "<stdin>", line 1
    ax.plot_surface(X, Y, Z, rstride=1, cstride=1, cmap=cm.plasma,
    linewidth=0, antialiased=False)
    ^
IndentationError: unexpected indent
>>>     plt.savefig('rastrigin.png')
  File "<stdin>", line 1
    plt.savefig('rastrigin.png')
    ^
IndentationError: unexpected indent
>>> if __name__ == '__main__':
...     X = np.linspace(-4, 4, 200)
...     Y = np.linspace(-4, 4, 200)
...
>>> X, Y = np.meshgrid(X, Y)
>>> Z = rastrigin(X, Y, A=10)
>>> fig = plt.figure()
```

```
>>> ax = fig.gca(projection='3d')
>>> ax.plot_surface(X, Y, Z, rstride=1, cstride=1, cmap=cm.plasma,
linewidth=0, antialiased=False)
<mpl_toolkits.mplot3d.art3d.Poly3DCollection object at 0x7f79cfc73780>
>>> plt.savefig('rastrigin.png')
>>>
```

If you go back to the folder, you can see that the rastrigin.png file was created, as shown in Figure 4-24.

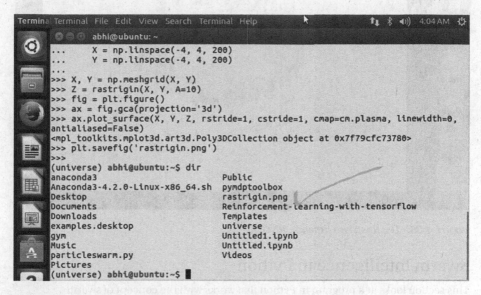

Figure 4-24. *Rastrigin function PNG file being saved*

The rastrigin.png file's output from the problem shows the minima, as shown in Figure 4-25. It is very difficult to find the global optimum.

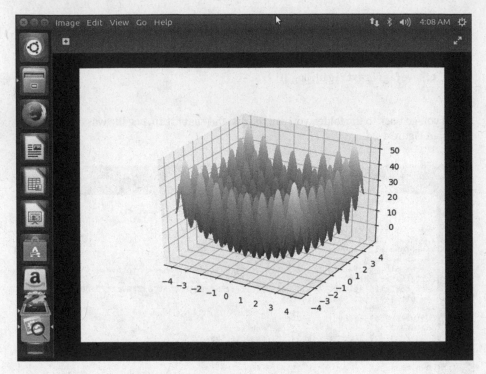

Figure 4-25. *The Rastrigin function PNG file*

Swarm Intelligence in Python

This section looks at a program in Python that works with the concept of swarm intelligence. You will therefore get to know particle swarm optimization (PSO) within Python. You can achieve this with the help of a research toolkit known as *PySwarms*.

PySwarms is a good tool to implement optimization algorithms with the PSO method, such as:

- Star topology

- Ring topology

First, you need to install PySwarms. Get inside the terminal and activate the Anaconda environment using the following command.

```
abhi@ubuntu:~$ source activate universe
(universe) abhi@ubuntu:~$
```

The dependencies prior to installing PySwarms are as follows:

```
numpy >= 1.13.0
scipy >= 0.17.0
matplotlib >= 1.3.1
```

Now install PySwarms as follows:

```
(universe) abhi@ubuntu:~$ pip install pyswarms
```

Now the process is complete.
Figure 4-26 shows that PySwarms is completely installed.

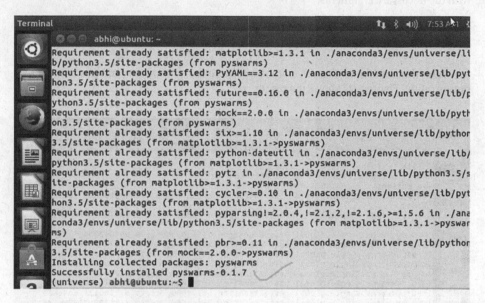

Figure 4-26. *PySwarms are installed*

Now we move to Python mode.

```
(universe) abhi@ubuntu:~$ python
Python 3.5.3 |Anaconda custom (64-bit)| (default, Mar  6 2017, 11:58:13)
[GCC 4.4.7 20120313 (Red Hat 4.4.7-1)] on linux
Type "help", "copyright", "credits" or "license" for more information.
>>>
```

First, you need to import the PySwarms utilities as follows:

```
>>> import pyswarms as ps
```

There are different functions that you can use in PySwarms for that you have to import:

```
>>> from pyswarms.utils.functions import single_obj as fx
```

Next, you need to declare these hyperparameters:

```
>>> options = {'c1': 0.5, 'c2': 0.3, 'w':0.9}
```

In this case, we are configuring the swarm as a dictionary, so call it a dictionary.

In the next step, you create the instance of the optimizer by passing the dictionary with the necessary arguments.

```
>>> optimizer = ps.single.GlobalBestPSO(n_particles=10, dimensions=2,
options=options)
```

After that, call the `optimizer` method and store the optimal cost and position after optimization. Figure 4-27 shows the results.

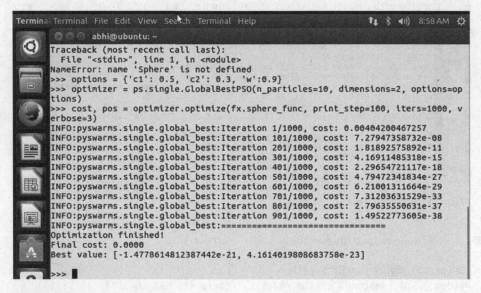

Figure 4-27. Showing the result

After going through the results, you can see that `optimizer` was able to find a good minima.

You will now do the same using the local best PSO. You configure and similarly declare a dictionary as follows:

```
>>> options = {'c1': 0.5, 'c2': 0.3, 'w':0.9, 'k': 2, 'p': 2}
```

Create the instance of the optimizer:

```
>>> optimizer = ps.single.LocalBestPSO(n_particles=10, dimensions=2,
options=options)
```

Now you call the `optimize` method to store the value as you did before.

By using the `verbose` argument, you can control the verbosity of the argument and use `print_step` to count after a certain number of steps.

```
>>> cost, pos = optimizer.optimize(fx.sphere_func, print_step=50,
iters=1000, verbose=3)
```

The output is shown in Figure 4-28.

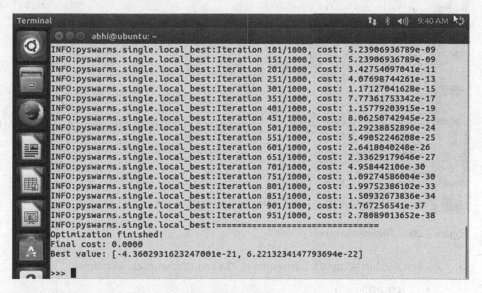

Figure 4-28. *The output of the swarm optimization*

Building a Game AI

We have already discussed the game AI with OpenAI Gym and environment simulation, but we take it further in this section. First, we will clone one of the most important and simplest examples of game AI, as shown in Figure 4-29.

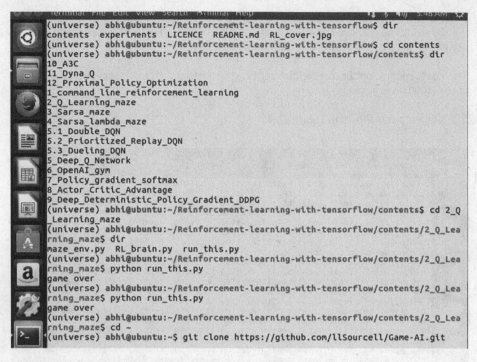

Figure 4-29. *Cloning the repo*

You first need to set up the environment. The requirements are as follows:

- TensorFlow

- OpenAI Gym

- virtualenv

- TFLearn

There is one dependency to install—the virtual environment. You install it using this command:

```
conda install -c anaconda virtualenv
```

It will ask you whether you want to install the new virtualenv package, as shown in Figure 4-30. Choose yes.

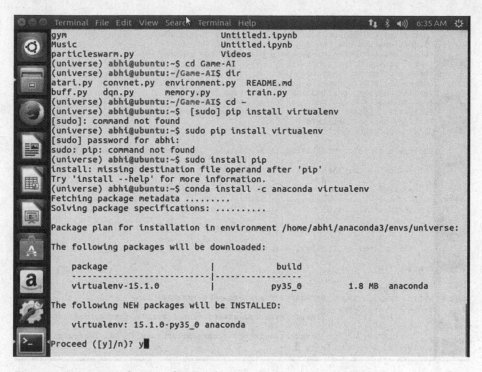

Figure 4-30. *Getting the virtualenv package*

When the package installation is successful and complete, you'll see the screen in Figure 4-31.

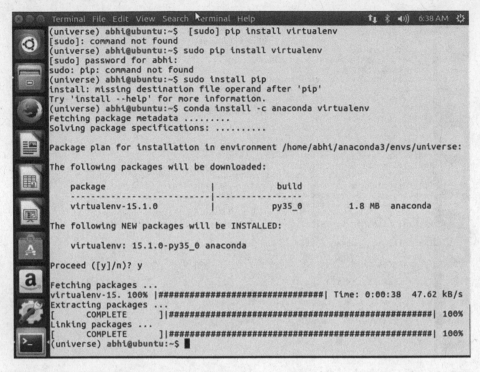

Figure 4-31. *Package installation is complete*

Now you can install TFLearn using this command:

```
conda install -c derickl tflearn
```

When you attempt to install TFLearn, you may get this error about an OS version mismatch:

```
conda install -c derickl tflearn
Fetching package metadata .........
Solving package specifications: .
PackageNotFoundError: Package not found: '' Package missing in current
linux-64 channels:
  - tflearn
You can search for packages on anaconda.org with
    anaconda search -t conda tflearn
(universe) abhi@ubuntu:~$ anaconda search -t conda tflearn
Using Anaconda API: https://api.anaconda.org
Run 'anaconda show <USER/PACKAGE>' to get more details:
```

```
Packages:
    Name                         | Version | Package Types   | Platforms
    -------------------------    | ------  | --------------- | -------------
--
    asherp/tflearn               |  0.2.2  | conda           | osx-64
    contango/tflearn             |  0.3.2  | conda           | linux-64
    derickl/tflearn              |  0.2.2  | conda           | osx-64
Found 3 packages
```

If this happens, be sure to install the one that's for linux-64:

```
(universe) abhi@ubuntu:~$ anaconda show contango/tflearn
Using Anaconda API: https://api.anaconda.org
Name:    tflearn
Summary:
Access: public
Package Types: conda
Versions:
   + 0.3.2
```

To install this package with Anaconda, run the following command:

```
conda install --channel https://conda.anaconda.org/contango tflearn
```

It will ask for installation of other packages, as shown in Figure 4-32.

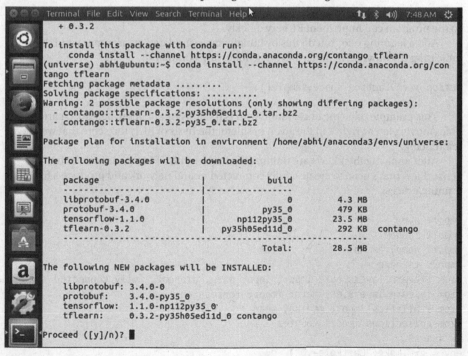

Figure 4-32. *Installation of other packages*

Now import the relevant libraries using this command:

```
(universe) abhi@ubuntu:~$ python
Python 3.5.3 |Anaconda custom (64-bit)| (default, Mar  6 2017, 11:58:13)
[GCC 4.4.7 20120313 (Red Hat 4.4.7-1)] on linux
Type "help", "copyright", "credits" or "license" for more information.
>>> import gym
>>> import random
>>> import numpy as np
>>> import tflearn
>>> from tflearn.layers.core import input_data, dropout, fully_connected
>>> from tflearn.layers.estimator import regression
>>> from statistics import median, mean
>>> from collections import Counter
>>> LR = 1e-3
>>> env = gym.make("CartPole-v0")
[2017-09-22 08:22:15,933] Making new env: CartPole-v0
>>> env.reset()
array([-0.03283849, -0.04877971,  0.0408221 , -0.01600674])
```

The Entire TFLearn Code

To start with, you need to import the important libraries. TFLearn creates the prototyping so the program can implement RL very quickly.

Add a learning rate. You do this by initializing a simulated environment and then indicating the movement pattern with the following command:

```
action = env.action_space.sample()
```

This example pairs the observation with is the movement of the balanced cart-pole (moving left or right). In the given problem, the basis of RL is the score that we are referencing.

After applying the RL, we are training the model with TFLearn, a module for TensorFlow that's used to create a fully connected neural network and produce a faster training process.

```
import gym
import random
import numpy as np
import tflearn
from tflearn.layers.core import input_data, dropout, fully_connected
from tflearn.layers.estimator import regression
from statistics import median, mean
from collections import Counter
LR = 1e-3
env = gym.make("CartPole-v0")
```

```python
env.reset()
goal_steps = 500
score_requirement = 50
initial_games = 10000
def some_random_games_first():
    # Each of these is its own game.
    for episode in range(5):
        env.reset()
        # this is each frame, up to 200...but we wont make it that far.
        for t in range(200):
            # This will display the environment
            # Only display if you really want to see it.
            # Takes much longer to display it.
            env.render()

            # This will just create a sample action in any environment.
            # In this environment, the action can be 0 or 1, which is left
            #   or right
            action = env.action_space.sample()

            # this executes the environment with an action,
            # and returns the observation of the environment,
            # the reward, if the env is over, and other info.
            observation, reward, done, info = env.step(action)
            if done:
                break

some_random_games_first()
def initial_population():
    # [OBS, MOVES]
    training_data = []
    # all scores:
    scores = []
    # just the scores that met our threshold:
    accepted_scores = []
    # iterate through however many games we want:
    for _ in range(initial_games):
        score = 0
        # moves specifically from this environment:
        game_memory = []
        # previous observation that we saw
        prev_observation = []
        # for each frame in 200
        for _ in range(goal_steps):
            # choose random action (0 or 1)
            action = random.randrange(0,2)
            # do it!
            observation, reward, done, info = env.step(action)
```

```
                    # notice that the observation is returned FROM the action
                    # so we'll store the previous observation here, pairing
                    # the prev observation to the action we'll take.
                    if len(prev_observation) > 0 :
                        game_memory.append([prev_observation, action])
                    prev_observation = observation
                    score+=reward
                    if done: break
            # IF our score is higher than our threshold, we'd like to save
            # every move we made
            # NOTE the reinforcement methodology here.
            # all we're doing is reinforcing the score, we're not trying
            # to influence the machine in any way as to HOW that score is
            # reached.
            if score >= score_requirement:
                accepted_scores.append(score)
                for data in game_memory:
                    # convert to one-hot (this is the output layer for our
                      neural network)
                    if data[1] == 1:
                        output = [0,1]
                    elif data[1] == 0:
                        output = [1,0]

                    # saving our training data
                    training_data.append([data[0], output])
            # reset env to play again
            env.reset()
            # save overall scores
            scores.append(score)

    # just in case you wanted to reference later
    training_data_save = np.array(training_data)
    np.save('saved.npy',training_data_save)

    # some stats here, to further illustrate the neural network magic!
    print('Average accepted score:',mean(accepted_scores))
    print('Median score for accepted scores:',median(accepted_scores))
    print(Counter(accepted_scores))

    return training_data
def neural_network_model(input_size):
    network = input_data(shape=[None, input_size, 1], name='input')
    network = fully_connected(network, 128, activation='relu')
    network = dropout(network, 0.8)
    network = fully_connected(network, 256, activation='relu')
    network = dropout(network, 0.8)
    network = fully_connected(network, 512, activation='relu')
```

```
    network = dropout(network, 0.8)
    network = fully_connected(network, 256, activation='relu')
    network = dropout(network, 0.8)
    network = fully_connected(network, 128, activation='relu')
    network = dropout(network, 0.8)
    network = fully_connected(network, 2, activation='softmax')
    network = regression(network, optimizer='adam', learning_rate=LR,
    loss='categorical_crossentropy', name='targets')
    model = tflearn.DNN(network, tensorboard_dir='log')
    return model
def train_model(training_data, model=False):
    X = np.array([i[0] for i in training_data]).reshape(-1,len(training_
    data[0][0]),1)
    y = [i[1] for i in training_data]
    if not model:
        model = neural_network_model(input_size = len(X[0]))
        x = np.reshape(x, (-1, 30, 9))

    model.fit({'input': X}, {'targets': y}, n_epoch=5, snapshot_step=500,
    show_metric=True, run_id='openai_learning')
    return model
    model = train_model(training_data)
    scores = []
choices = []
for each_game in range(10):
    score = 0
    game_memory = []
    prev_obs = []
    env.reset()
    for _ in range(goal_steps):
        env.render()
        if len(prev_obs)==0:
            action = random.randrange(0,2)
        else:
            action = np.argmax(model.predict(prev_obs.reshape(-1,len(prev_
            obs),1))[0])
        choices.append(action)

        new_observation, reward, done, info = env.step(action)
        prev_obs = new_observation
        game_memory.append([new_observation, action])
        score+=reward
        if done: break
    scores.append(score)
print('Average Score:',sum(scores)/len(scores))
print('choice 1:{}  choice 0:{}'.format(choices.count(1)/
len(choices),choices.count(0)/len(choices)))
print(score_requirement)
```

Here is the output:

```
Average Score: 195.9
choice 1:0.5074017355793773   choice 0:0.49259826442062277
50
Solved.
```

Conclusion

This chapter touched on Q learning and then showed some examples. It also covered the MDP toolbox, swarm intelligence, and game AI, and ended with a full example. Chapter 5 covers Reinforcement Learning with Keras, TensorFlow, and ChainerRL.

CHAPTER 5

■ ■ ■

Reinforcement Learning with Keras, TensorFlow, and ChainerRL

This chapter covers using Keras with Reinforcement Learning and defines how Keras can be used for Deep Q Learning as well.

What Is Keras?

Keras is an open source frontend library for neural networks. We can say that it works as a backbone for the neural network, as it has very good capabilities for forming activation functions. Keras can run different deep learning frameworks as the backend.

Keras runs with lots of deep learning frameworks. The way to change from one framework to another is to modify the keras.json file, which is located in the same directory where Keras is installed.

The backend parameter needs to change as follows:

```
{
"backend" : "tensorflow"
}
```

You can change the parameter from TensorFlow to another framework if you want.

In the JSON file, if you want to use it with Theano or CNTK, you can do so by changing the backend parameter.

The structure of a keras.json file looks like this:

```
{
    "image_data_format": "channels_last",
    "epsilon": 1e-07,
    "floatx": "float32",
    "backend": "tensorflow"
}
```

© Abhishek Nandy and Manisha Biswas 2018
A. Nandy and M. Biswas, *Reinforcement Learning*,
https://doi.org/10.1007/978-1-4842-3285-9_5

The flow of all the Keras frameworks is shown in Figure 5-1.

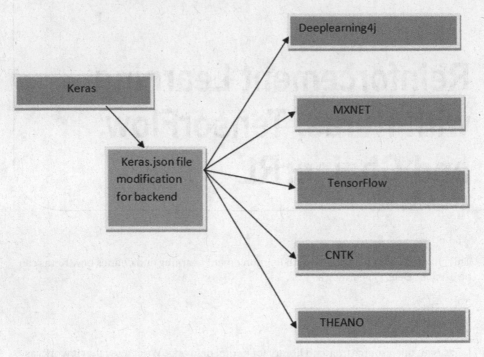

Figure 5-1. *Keras and its modification with different frameworks*

Using Keras for Reinforcement Learning

This section covers installing Keras and shows an example of Reinforcement Learning. You first need to install the dependencies.

The dependencies are as follows:

- Python

- Keras 1.0

- Pygame

- Scikit-image

Let's start installing Keras 1.0. This example shows how to install Keras from the Anaconda environment:

```
conda install -c jaikumarm keras
```

It asks for permission to install the new packages. Choose yes to proceed, as shown in Figure 5-2.

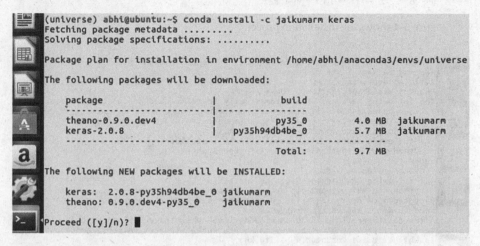

Figure 5-2. *The updates to be installed*

When the package installation is successful and completed, you'll see the information shown in Figure 5-3.

```
Proceed ([y]/n)? y

Fetching packages ...
theano-0.9.0.d 100% |###############################| Time: 0:01:07  61.88 kB/s
keras-2.0.8-py 100% |###############################| Time: 0:01:29  67.55 kB/s
Extracting packages ...
[         COMPLETE         ]|#################################################| 100%
Linking packages ...
[         COMPLETE         ]|#################################################| 100%
(universe) abhi@ubuntu:~$
```

Figure 5-3. *The package installation is complete*

You can also install Keras in a different way too. This example shows you how to install it using pip3.

First, use sudo apt update as follows:

```
(universe) abhi@ubuntu:~$ sudo apt-get update
```

Then install pip3 as follows:

```
sudo apt-get -y install python3-pip
```

Figure 5-4 shows the installation process.

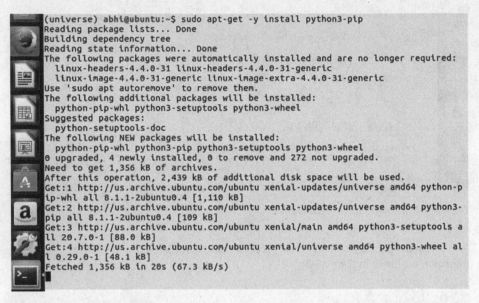

Figure 5-4. *Installing pip3*

After the dependencies, you need to install Keras (see Figure 5-5):

```
(universe) abhi@ubuntu:~$ sudo pip3 install keras
```

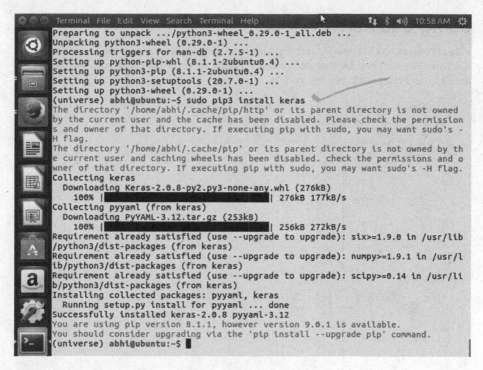

Figure 5-5. Installing Keras

We will check now if Keras uses the TensorFlow backend or not. From the terminal Anaconda environment you enabled first, you need to switch to Python mode.

If you get the following result importing Keras, that means everything is working (see Figure 5-6).

```
(universe) abhi@ubuntu:~$ python
Python 3.5.3 |Anaconda custom (64-bit)| (default, Mar  6 2017, 11:58:13)
[GCC 4.4.7 20120313 (Red Hat 4.4.7-1)] on linux
Type "help", "copyright", "credits" or "license" for more information.
>>> import keras
Using TensorFlow backend.
```

```
(universe) abhi@ubuntu:~$ python
Python 3.5.3 |Anaconda custom (64-bit)| (default, Mar  6 2017, 11:58:13)
[GCC 4.4.7 20120313 (Red Hat 4.4.7-1)] on linux
Type "help", "copyright", "credits" or "license" for more information.
>>> import keras
Using TensorFlow backend.
>>>
```

Figure 5-6. Keras with the TensorFlow backend

133

Using ChainerRL

This section covers ChainerRL and explains how to apply Reinforcement Learning using it. ChainerRL is a deep Reinforcement Learning library especially built with the help of the Chainer Framework. See Figure 5-7.

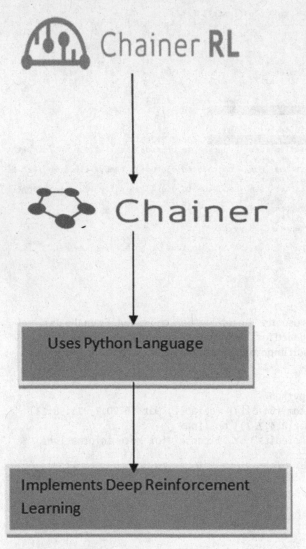

Figure 5-7. ChainerRL

Installing ChainerRL

We will install ChainerRL first from the terminal window. Figure 5-8 shows the Anaconda environment.

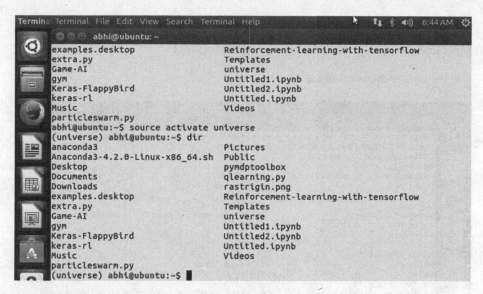

Figure 5-8. *Activating the Anaconda environment*

You can now install ChainerRL. To do so, type this command in the terminal:

```
pip install chainerrl
```

Figure 5-9 shows the result of the installation.

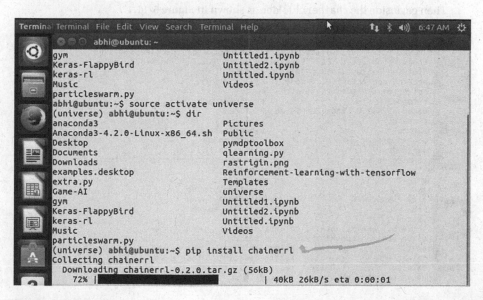

Figure 5-9. *Installing ChainerRL*

Now you can git clone the repo. Use this command to do so:

```
git clone https://github.com/chainer/chainerrl.git
```

Figure 5-10 shows the result.

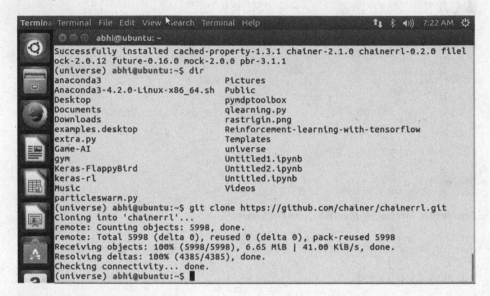

Figure 5-10. *Cloning ChainerRL*

Then get inside the chainerrl folder, as shown in Figure 5-11.

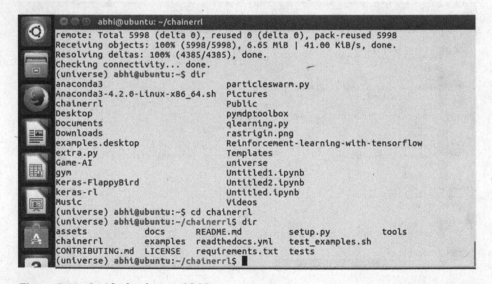

Figure 5-11. *Inside the chainerrl folder*

Pipeline for Using ChainerRL

Since the library is based on Python, the obvious language of choice is Python. Follow these steps to set up ChainerRL:

1. Import the gym, numpy, and supportive chainerrl libraries.

```
import chainer
import chainer.functions as F
import chainer.links as L
import chainerrl
import gym
import numpy as np
```

You have to model an environment so that you can use OpenAI Gym (see Figure 5-12). The environment has two spaces:

- Observation space

- Action space

They must have two methods, reset and step.

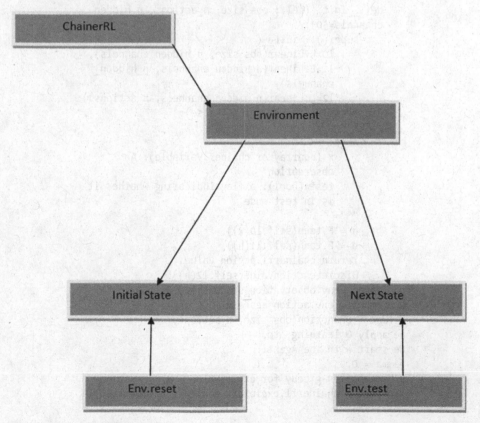

Figure 5-12. *How ChainerRL uses state transitions*

2. Take a simulation environment such as `Cartpole-v0` from the OpenAI simulation environment.

```python
env = gym.make('CartPole-v0')
print('observation space:', env.observation_space)
print('action space:', env.action_space)
obs = env.reset()
env.render()
print('initial observation:', obs)
action = env.action_space.sample()
obs, r, done, info = env.step(action)
print('next observation:', obs)
print('reward:', r)
print('done:', done)
print('info:', info)
```

3. Now define an agent that will run from interactions with the environment. Here, it's the `QFunction(chainer.Chain)` class:

```python
    def __init__(self, obs_size, n_actions, n_hidden_
    channels=50):
        super().__init__(
            l0=L.Linear(obs_size, n_hidden_channels),
            l1=L.Linear(n_hidden_channels, n_hidden_
            channels),
            l2=L.Linear(n_hidden_channels, n_actions))
    def __call__(self, x, test=False):
        """
        Args:
            x (ndarray or chainer.Variable): An
            observation
            test (bool): a flag indicating whether it
            is in test mode
        """

        h = F.tanh(self.l0(x))
        h = F.tanh(self.l1(h))
        return chainerrl.action_value.
        DiscreteActionValue(self.l2(h))
obs_size = env.observation_space.shape[0]
n_actions = env.action_space.n
q_func = QFunction(obs_size, n_actions)
we apply Q learning etc.
We start with the Agent.
gamma = 0.95
# Use epsilon-greedy for exploration
explorer = chainerrl.explorers.ConstantEpsilonGreedy(
```

```
        epsilon=0.3, random_action_func=env.action_space.
        sample)
    # DQN uses Experience Replay.
    # Specify a replay buffer and its capacity.
    replay_buffer = chainerrl.replay_buffer.
    ReplayBuffer(capacity=10 ** 6)
    # Since observations from CartPole-v0 is numpy.float64
    while
    # Chainer only accepts numpy.float32 by default,
    specify
    # a converter as a feature extractor function phi.
    phi = lambda x: x.astype(np.float32, copy=False)
    # Now create an agent that will interact with the
    environment.
    agent = chainerrl.agents.DoubleDQN(
        q_func, optimizer, replay_buffer, gamma, explorer,
        replay_start_size=500, update_interval=1,
        target_update_interval=100, phi=phi)
```

4. Start the Reinforcement Learning process. You have to open
    the jupyter notebook first in the Universe environment, as
    shown in Figure 5-13.

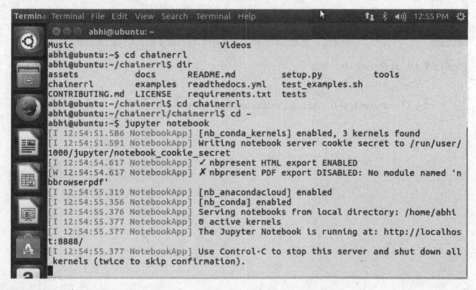

Figure 5-13. *Getting inside jupyter notebook*

```
abhi@ubuntu:~$ source activate universe
(universe) abhi@ubuntu:~$ jupyter notebook
```

Figure 5-14 shows running the code on the final go.

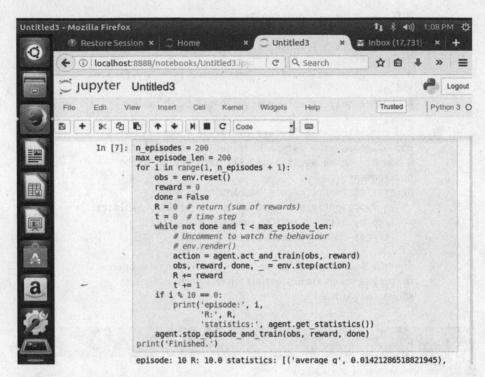

Figure 5-14. *Running the code*

5.   Now you test the agents, as shown in Figure 5-15.

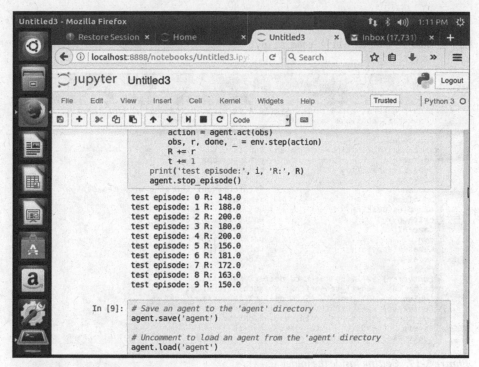

Figure 5-15. Testing the agents

We completed the entire program in the jupyter notebook. Now we will work on one of the repos for understanding Deep Q Learning with TensorFlow. See Figure 5-16.

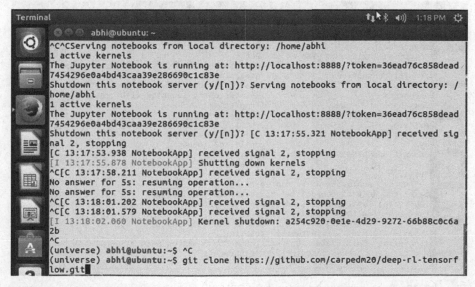

Figure 5-16. Cloning the GitHub repo

First you need to install the prerequisites as follows (see Figure 5-17):

```
pip install -U 'gym[all]' tqdm scipy
```

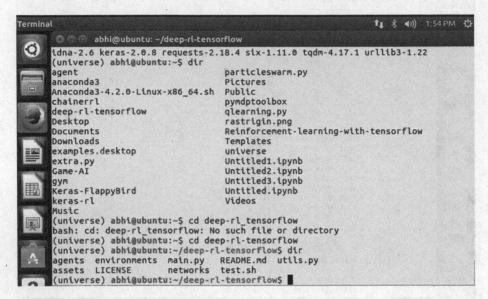

Figure 5-17. *Getting inside the folder*

Then run the program and train it without using GPU support, as shown in Figure 5-18.

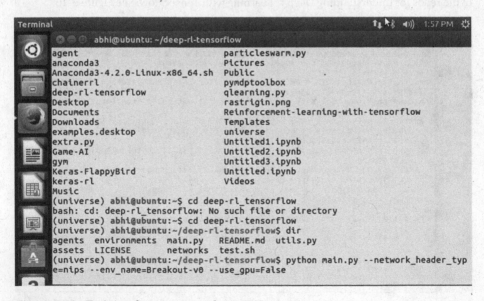

Figure 5-18. *Training the program without GPU support*

The command is as follows:

```
$ python main.py --network_header_type=nips --env_name=Breakout-v0 --use_
gpu=False
```

The command uses the `main.py` Python file and runs the Breakout game simulation in CPU mode only. You can now open the terminal to get inside the Anaconda environment, as shown in Figure 5-19.

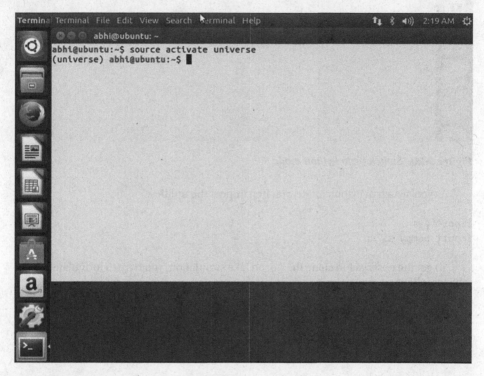

Figure 5-19. *Activating the environment*

Now switch to Python mode, as shown in Figure 5-20:

```
(universe) abhi@ubuntu:~$ python
Python 3.5.3 |Anaconda custom (64-bit)| (default, Mar  6 2017, 11:58:13)
[GCC 4.4.7 20120313 (Red Hat 4.4.7-1)] on linux
Type "help", "copyright", "credits" or "license" for more information.
>>>
```

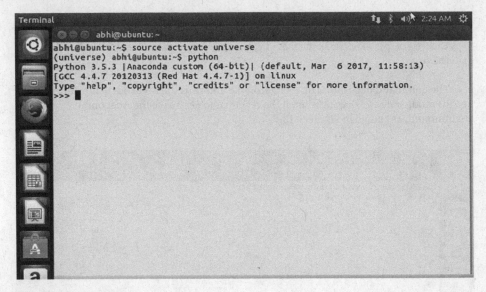

Figure 5-20. *Switching to Python mode*

As you switch to Python mode, you first import the utilities:

```
import gym
import numpy as np
```

To get the observation along the frozen lake simulation, you have to formulate the Q table as follows:

```
Q = np.zeros([env.observation_space.n,env.action_space.n])
```

After that, you declare the learning rates and create the lists to contain the rewards for each state.

```
import gym
import numpy as np
env = gym.make('FrozenLake-v0')
#Initialize table with all zeros
Q = np.zeros([env.observation_space.n,env.action_space.n])
# Set learning parameters
lr = .8
y = .95
num_episodes = 2000
#create lists to contain total rewards and steps per episode
#jList = []
rList = []
for i in range(num_episodes):
```

```
#Reset environment and get first new observation
s = env.reset()
rAll = 0
d = False
j = 0
#The Q-Table learning algorithm
while j < 99:
    j+=1
    #Choose an action by greedily (with noise) picking from Q table
    a = np.argmax(Q[s,:] + np.random.randn(1,env.action_space.n)*
    (1./(i+1)))
    #Get new state and reward from environment
    s1,r,d,_ = env.step(a)
    #Update Q-Table with new knowledge
    Q[s,a] = Q[s,a] + lr*(r + y*np.max(Q[s1,:]) - Q[s,a])
    rAll += r
    s = s1
    if d == True:
        break
#jList.append(j)
rList.append(rAll)
print "Score over time: " +  str(sum(rList)/num_episodes)
print "Final Q-Table Values"
print Q
```

After going through all the steps, you can finally print the Q table. Each line should be placed into Python mode.

Deep Q Learning: Using Keras and TensorFlow

We will touch on Deep Q Learning with Keras. We will clone an important reinforcement library, which is known as Keras-rl. It has several states of the Deep Q Learning algorithms. See Figure 5-21.

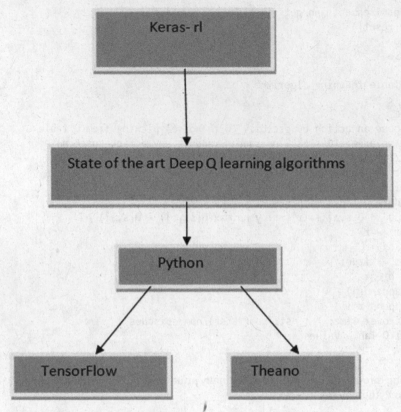

Figure 5-21. *Keras-rl representation*

Installing Keras-rl

The command for installing Keras-rl is as follows (see Figure 5-22):

```
pip install keras-rl
```

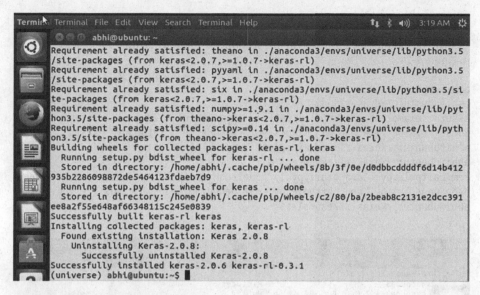

Figure 5-22. *Installing Keras-rl*

You also need to install h5py if it is not already installed and then you need to clone the repo, as shown in Figure 5-23.

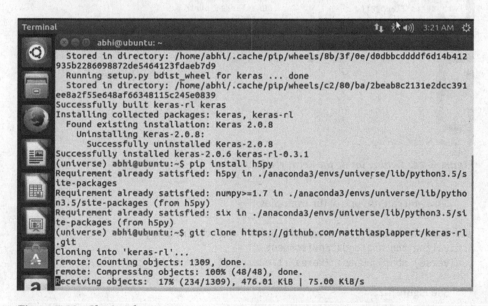

Figure 5-23. *Cloning the git repo*

Training with Keras-rl

You will see how to run a program in this section. First, get inside the rl folder, as shown in Figure 5-24.

```
abhi@ubuntu:~$ cd keras-rl
abhi@ubuntu:~/keras-rl$ dir
assets   examples          LICENSE    pytest.ini  rl          setup.py
docs     ISSUE_TEMPLATE.md mkdocs.yml README.md   setup.cfg   tests
abhi@ubuntu:~/keras-rl$ cd examples
abhi@ubuntu:~/keras-rl/examples$ dir
cem_cartpole.py   dqn_atari.py       duel_dqn_cartpole.py  sarsa_cartpole.py
ddpg_pendulum.py  dqn_cartpole.py    naf_pendulum.py       visualize_log.py
abhi@ubuntu:~/keras-rl/examples$
```

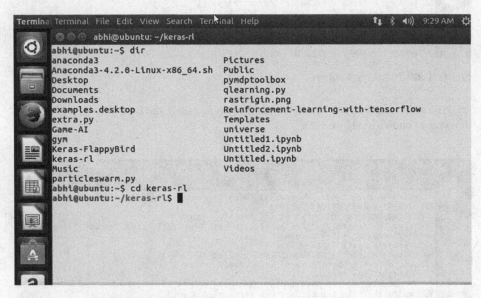

Figure 5-24. *Getting inside the Keras-rl directory*

Now you can run one of the examples:

```
abhi@ubuntu:~/keras-rl/examples$ python dqn_cartpole.py
Activating the anaconda environment
(universe) abhi@ubuntu:~/keras-rl/examples$ python dqn_cartpole.py
```

See Figure 5-25.

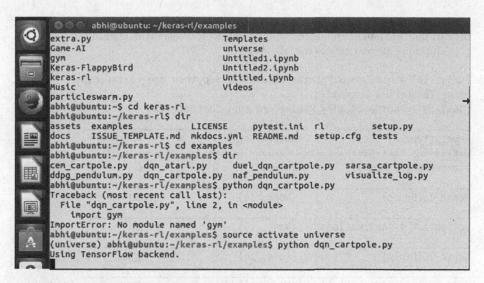

Figure 5-25. *Using the TensorFlow backend*

The simulation will now begin, as shown in Figure 5-26.

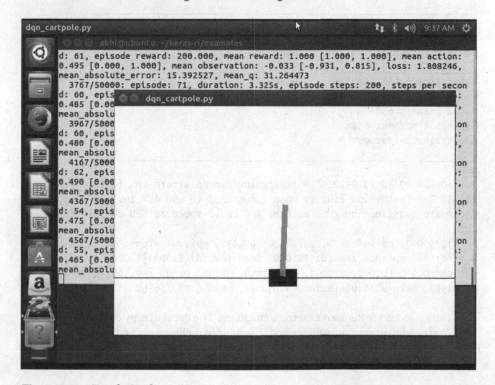

Figure 5-26. *Simulation happens*

The simulation occurs and trains the model using Deep Q Learning. With practice, the cart-pole will balance along the rope; its stability increases with learning.

The entire process creates the following log:

```
(universe) abhi@ubuntu:~/keras-rl/examples$ python dqn_cartpole.py
Using TensorFlow backend.
[2017-09-24 09:36:27,476] Making new env: CartPole-v0
```

Layer (type)	Output Shape	Param #
flatten_1 (Flatten)	(None, 4)	0
dense_1 (Dense)	(None, 16)	80
activation_1 (Activation)	(None, 16)	0
dense_2 (Dense)	(None, 16)	272
activation_2 (Activation)	(None, 16)	0
dense_3 (Dense)	(None, 16)	272
activation_3 (Activation)	(None, 16)	0
dense_4 (Dense)	(None, 2)	34
activation_4 (Activation)	(None, 2)	0

```
Total params: 658
Trainable params: 658
Non-trainable params: 0
```

```
None
2017-09-24 09:36:27.932219: W tensorflow/core/platform/cpu_feature_guard.
cc:45] The TensorFlow library wasn't compiled to use AVX instructions, but
these are available on your machine and could speed up CPU computations.
...
   712/50000: episode: 38, duration: 0.243s, episode steps: 14, steps per
second: 58, episode reward: 14.000, mean reward: 1.000 [1.000, 1.000], mean
action: 0.500 [0.000, 1.000], mean observation: 0.105 [-0.568, 0.957], loss:
0.291389, mean_absolute_error: 3.054634, mean_q: 5.816398
```

The episodes are iterations for the simulations. The cartpole.py code is discussed next. You need to import the utilities first. The utilities included are very useful, as they have built-in agents for applying Deep Q Learning.

First, declare the environment as follows:

```
ENV_NAME = 'CartPole-v0'
env = gym.make(ENV_NAME)
```

Since we want to implement Deep Q Learning, we use parameters for initializing the Convolution Neural Network (CNN). We also use an activation function to propagate the neural network. We keep it sequential.

```
model = Sequential()
model.add(Flatten(input_shape=(1,) + env.observation_space.shape))
model.add(Dense(16))
model.add(Activation('relu'))
model.add(Dense(16))
model.add(Activation('relu'))
model.add(Dense(16))
model.add(Activation('relu'))
model.add(Dense(nb_actions))
model.add(Activation('linear'))
```

You can print the model details too, as follows:

```
print(model.summary())
```

Next, configure the model and use all the Reinforcement Learning options with the help of a function.

```
import numpy as np
import gym
from keras.models import Sequential
from keras.layers import Dense, Activation, Flatten
from keras.optimizers import Adam
from rl.agents.dqn import DQNAgent
from rl.policy import BoltzmannQPolicy
from rl.memory import SequentialMemory
ENV_NAME = 'CartPole-v0'
# Get the environment and extract the number of actions.
env = gym.make(ENV_NAME)
np.random.seed(123)
env.seed(123)
nb_actions = env.action_space.n
# Next, we build a very simple model.
model = Sequential()
model.add(Flatten(input_shape=(1,) + env.observation_space.shape))
model.add(Dense(16))
model.add(Activation('relu'))
model.add(Dense(16))
model.add(Activation('relu'))
model.add(Dense(16))
model.add(Activation('relu'))
model.add(Dense(nb_actions))
model.add(Activation('linear'))
print(model.summary())
```

```
# Finally, we configure and compile our agent. You can use every built-in
Keras optimizer and
# even the metrics!
memory = SequentialMemory(limit=50000, window_length=1)
policy = BoltzmannQPolicy()
dqn = DQNAgent(model=model, nb_actions=nb_actions, memory=memory, nb_steps_
warmup=10,
                target_model_update=1e-2, policy=policy)
dqn.compile(Adam(lr=1e-3), metrics=['mae'])
# Okay, now it's time to learn something! We visualize the training here for
show, but this
# slows down training quite a lot. You can always safely abort the training
prematurely using
# Ctrl + C.
dqn.fit(env, nb_steps=50000, visualize=True, verbose=2)
# After training is done, we save the final weights.
dqn.save_weights('dqn_{}_weights.h5f'.format(ENV_NAME), overwrite=True)
# Finally, evaluate our algorithm for 5 episodes.
dqn.test(env, nb_episodes=5, visualize=True)
```

To get all the capabilities of Keras-rl, you need to run the setup.py file within the Keras-rl folder, as follows:

```
(universe) abhi@ubuntu:~/keras-rl$ python setup.py install
```

You will see that all the dependencies are being installed, one by one:

```
running install
running bdist_egg
running egg_info
creating keras_rl.egg-info
writing requirements to keras_rl.egg-info/requires.txt
writing dependency_links to keras_rl.egg-info/dependency_links.txt
writing top-level names to keras_rl.egg-info/top_level.txt
writing keras_rl.egg-info/PKG-INFO
writing manifest file 'keras_rl.egg-info/SOURCES.txt'
reading manifest file 'keras_rl.egg-info/SOURCES.txt'
writing manifest file 'keras_rl.egg-info/SOURCES.txt'
installing library code to build/bdist.linux-x86_64/egg
running install_lib
running build_py
creating build
creating build/lib
creating build/lib/tests
copying tests/__init__.py -> build/lib/tests
creating build/lib/rl
copying rl/util.py -> build/lib/rl
copying rl/callbacks.py -> build/lib/rl
```

```
copying rl/keras_future.py -> build/lib/rl
copying rl/memory.py -> build/lib/rl
copying rl/random.py -> build/lib/rl
copying rl/core.py -> build/lib/rl
copying rl/__init__.py -> build/lib/rl
copying rl/policy.py -> build/lib/rl
creating build/lib/tests/rl
copying tests/rl/test_util.py -> build/lib/tests/rl
copying tests/rl/util.py -> build/lib/tests/rl
copying tests/rl/test_memory.py -> build/lib/tests/rl
copying tests/rl/test_core.py -> build/lib/tests/rl
copying tests/rl/__init__.py -> build/lib/tests/rl
creating build/lib/tests/rl/agents
copying tests/rl/agents/test_cem.py -> build/lib/tests/rl/agents
copying tests/rl/agents/__init__.py -> build/lib/tests/rl/agents
copying tests/rl/agents/test_ddpg.py -> build/lib/tests/rl/agents
copying tests/rl/agents/test_dqn.py -> build/lib/tests/rl/agents
creating build/lib/rl/agents
copying rl/agents/sarsa.py -> build/lib/rl/agents
copying rl/agents/ddpg.py -> build/lib/rl/agents
copying rl/agents/dqn.py -> build/lib/rl/agents
copying rl/agents/cem.py -> build/lib/rl/agents
copying rl/agents/__init__.py -> build/lib/rl/agents
```

Keras-rl is now set up and you can use the built-in functions to their fullest effect.

Conclusion

This chapter introduced and defined Keras and explained how to use it with Reinforcement Learning. The chapter also explained how to use TensorFlow with Reinforcement Learning and discussed using ChainerRL. Chapter 6 covers Google DeepMind and the future of Reinforcement Learning.

CHAPTER 6

■■■

Google's DeepMind and the Future of Reinforcement Learning

This chapter discusses Google DeepMind and Google AlphaGo and then moves on to the future of Reinforcement Learning and compares what's happening with man versus machine.

Google DeepMind

Google DeepMind (see Figure 6-1) was formed to take AI to the next level. The aim and motive of Google in this case is to research and develop programs that can solve complex problems without needing to teach it the steps for doing so.

Figure 6-1. *Google DeepMind logo*

A. Nandy and M. Biswas, *Reinforcement Learning*,
https://doi.org/10.1007/978-1-4842-3285-9_6

The link to visit the DeepMind web site is `https://deepmind.com/`.

This web site (see Figure 6-2) contains all the details and the future work they are doing. There are publications and research options available on the site.

Figure 6-2. *The DeepMind web site*

You will see that the web site has lots of topics to search and discover.

Google AlphaGo

This section takes a look at AlphaGo (see Figure 6-3), which is one of the best solutions from the Google DeepMind team.

Figure 6-3. *The Google AlphaGo logo*

What Is AlphaGo?

AlphaGo is the Google program that plays the game Go, which is a traditional abstract strategy board game for two players. The object of the game is to occupy more territory than your opponent. Figure 6-4 shows the Go game board.

Figure 6-4. *The Go board (Image courtesy of Jaro Larnos, https://www.flickr.com/ photos/jlarnos/, used under a CC-BY 2.0 license)*

Despite its simple rules, Go has more possible solutions than the number of atoms in the visible world!

The concept of the Go game and its underlying mathematical terms included are illustrated in Figure 6-5.

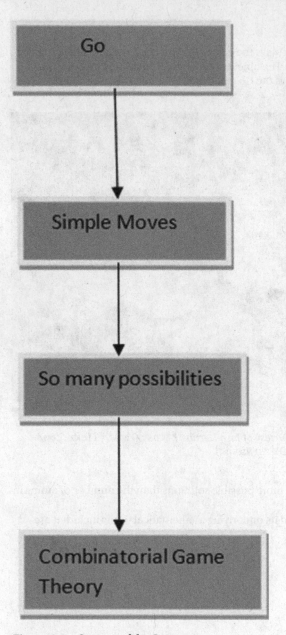

Figure 6-5. *Concept of the Go game*

AlphaGo is the first computer program to defeat a professional human Go player, the first program to defeat a Go world champion, and arguably the best Go player in history.

Figure 6-6 illustrates the AlphaGo approach.

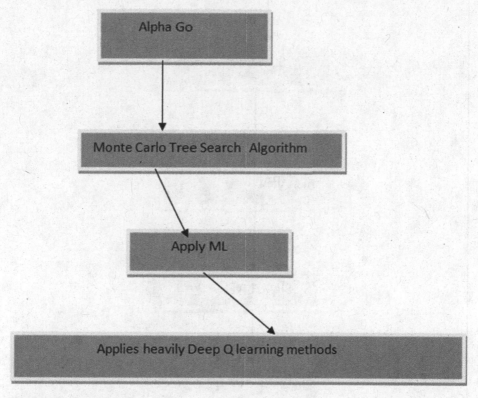

Figure 6-6. *Deep Q approach*

Monte Carlo Search

Monte Carlo Search (MCS) is based on the AI tree traversal approach. It uses a unique set of behaviors for moving through the tree.

MCS first selects each state it can go through, as mentioned in the declared policy. After a certain depth, the policy does not allow the state to go through. MCS then expands from that state to the possible actions that can be taken randomly. This way, you are using MCS-based simulation to all possible states to get rewards. We you do a random simulation path, you also get Q state values for random paths if you change from one state to another. From the Q state received, you can back up information and move to the top. The entire process is shown in Figure 6-7.

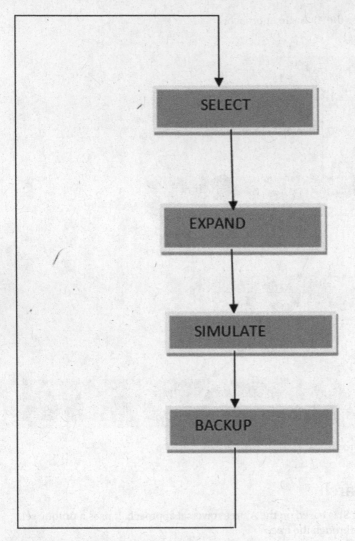

Figure 6-7. *The Monte Carlo Search tree process*

AlphaGo relies on two components: A tree search procedure and convolutional networks that guide the tree search procedure.

In total, three convolutional networks of two different kinds are trained: two policy networks and one value network.

Man vs. Machines

With the advent of Reinforcement Learning, there are many more jobs being automated and many low-level jobs are being done by machines.

Now the focus is on how Reinforcement Learning can solve different problems and change the well being of the earth.

For example, Reinforcement Learning can be used in the healthcare field. Instead of using the same age-old tools for body scans, we can train robots and medical equipment to scan body parts for different diagnoses purposes much quicker and with greater accuracy. With repeated training, decisions to perform more complex measurements and scans can be left to the machines too.

Positive Aspects of AI

Cognitive modeling is applied when we gather information and resources and through which the system learns. This is called the *cognitive way.* Technological singularity is achieved by enhancement of cognitive modeling devices that interact and achieve more unified goals.

A good strong AI solution is selfless and places the interest of others above all else. A good AI solution always works for the team. By adding human empathy, as seen with brainwaves, we can create good AI solutions that appear to be compassionate.

Applying a topological view to the world of AI helps streamline activities and allows each topology to master a specific, unique task.

Negative Aspects of AI

There can be negative aspects too. For example, what if a machine learns so fast that it starts talking to other machines and creates an AI of its own? In that case, it would be difficult for humans to predict the end game. We need to take these scenarios into consideration. Perhaps every AI solution needs a secret killswitch, as illustrated in Figure 6-8.

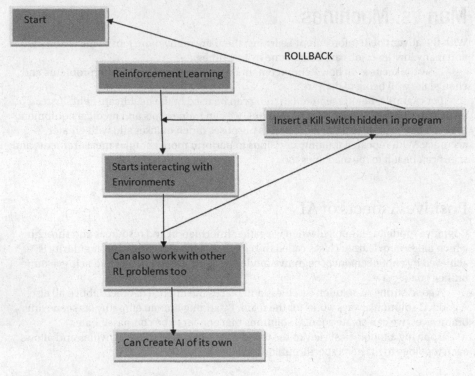

Figure 6-8. Insert a killswitch just in case

Here are the steps to this basic process:

1. We start a program.

2. We apply Machine Learning to it.

3. The program learns very quickly.

4. We have to incorporate a killswitch into the process so that we can allow the program to be rolled back if necessary.

5. When we see an anomaly or any abrupt behavior, we call the killswitch to roll the program back to the start.

There is a good chance that machines may learn this way, especially if they work in tandem. At some transition point, they might start interacting in a way that creates an AI of their own. We have to be able to avoid collisions of two or more Reinforcement Learning programs during the transition phase.

Conclusion

We touched on a lot of concepts in this book, especially related to Reinforcement Learning. The book is an overview of how Reinforcement Learning works and the ideas you need to understand to get started.

- We simplified the RL concepts with the help of the Python programming language.

- We introduced OpenAI Gym and OpenAI Universe.

- We introduced a lot of algorithms and touched on Keras and TensorFlow.

We hope you have liked the book. Thanks again!

Index

■ S, T, U, V, W, X, Y, Z

State Action Reward next State and next
Action (SARSA)
Q value, 56
temporal difference learning, 54–55
Swarm intelligence
ant-based routing, 110

crowd simulations, 110
human swarming, 110
interactions, 109
Python, 116–119
rastrigin
function, 111–116
swarm grammars, 111
swarmic art, 111

Get the eBook for only $5!

Why limit yourself?

With most of our titles available in both PDF and ePUB format, you can access your content wherever and however you wish—on your PC, phone, tablet, or reader.

Since you've purchased this print book, we are happy to offer you the eBook for just $5.

To learn more, go to http://www.apress.com/companion or contact support@apress.com.

Apress®

Printed in the United States
By Bookmasters